"Miss Wedgwood is completely at home with her material, her conception of her subject is broad and sound, her style is simple, direct and interesting. . . . The personality of Richelieu emerges forcefully in these pages—a strong man who had to operate in a political atmosphere that was often murky, and who, therefore, could not always show his hand." —*The American Historical Review*

"A generous and sympathetic portrayal of the powerful French Cardinal who built a powerful French monarchy from a corrupted and dying country"
—*Catholic Monthly Review*

Miss C. V. Wedgwood is an English historian who specializes in the seventeenth century. Her works include a biography of William the Silent, which was awarded the James Taite Black Memorial Prize, a biography of Oliver Cromwell, a history of the Thirty Years War, and several studies of the English Civil War.

Richelieu

and the French Monarchy

C. V. WEDGWOOD

NEW, REVISED EDITION

COLLIER BOOKS
A Division of Macmillan Publishing Co., Inc.

NEW YORK

Library of Congress Catalog Card Number: 62-19197
First Collier Books Edition 1962

16   15   14   13   12   11   10

Richelieu and the French Monarchy, *revised for Collier Books*, was published in a hardcover edition by Macmillan Publishing Co., Inc. This title first appeared as a volume in the *Teach Yourself History* series under the general editorship of A. L. Rowse.

Macmillan Publishing Co., Inc.
866 Third Avenue, New York, N.Y. 10022

ISBN 0-02-038240-5

Contents

Richelieu

Chapter 1

Richelieu and the French Monarchy

THIS BOOK is an account of a man's life. Armand Jean du Plessis, Cardinal Richelieu, was first minister of France for eighteen critical years (1624-1642) of the seventeenth century. During that time two things happened to France. First: the monarchy was established so firmly that even the long minority of Louis XIV and the series of rebellions known as the Fronde could not shake its foundation. Secondly, France became the dominating power on the continent of Europe, both in politics and in the arts.

Making every reasonable allowance for the impersonal forces which assisted these two developments, it is impossible not to allow a good deal of the credit for both of them to Cardinal Richelieu. The part played by the Great Man in history is usually overestimated; on the other hand the modern fashion for allowing no influence to the individual at all, and ascribing all historical developments to social or economic forces seems equally mistaken. If forces beyond individual control—the spiritual force of a great religious revival, the economic and social forces, driving France towards national consciousness and expansion—played an important part in the creation of the French monarchy, it is difficult to imagine quite how these forces

9

would have found expression under other guidance than that of Cardinal Richelieu. It is the measure of his greatness that it should be so difficult to imagine the growth of the French monarchy, or the development of Europe in the seventeenth century, without him.

The Cardinal was so formidable a personality that, in his lifetime, his influence was suspected everywhere. He was credited wrongly by the English with having provoked the Scots Wars of 1639 and 1640, and rightly by the Spaniards with organising the Portuguese and Catalan revolts of the same period. His spies and agents covered Europe no less than his police system covered France. In the imagination of his contemporaries he was the cunning spider seated all-powerful in the midst of an enormous web of intrigue.

We are more inclined today to recognise that such personalities are not necessarily the dominating forces of history, that beneath the spectacular achievements of an astute diplomat and perspicacious politician, the threads of millions of other lives make up the colour-pattern of a period. Richelieu indeed could not have done what he did but for opportunities which were a part of a more vast and complicated design. France could not have risen to dominate Europe had it not been for her tough, hard-working peasant population, the toilers in the vineyards and the olive fields, or for her industrious artisans, the men and women at the looms of Lyons and Tours, in the glassworks of Meaux; or for her hard-headed and thrifty bourgeoisie, the solid and calculating shopkeepers of a hundred provincial cities. The French monarchy could not have been consolidated without the general desire for stable government which was the outcome of increasing prosperity and the need for expansion.

Richelieu achieved only what it was necessary to achieve. Moreover he was not a creative statesman for he invented nothing new. Instead he selected, as occasion dictated, such elements as already existed in the French state, and strengthened these at the expense of others.

His greatness lay in his clear-sighted opposition to the hostile elements which checked the emergence of the French nation-state. Had France lacked, at this crucial moment in the national development, a statesman with a clear eye and a resolute will the history of Europe would have been different. A central European consolidation, either under Habsburg, or even under Swedish, dominion might have taken place. France, as a nation, might have broken down, as Germany broke down, on the fatal separation of classes or provinces. France, as a monarchy, might have decayed inwardly as Spain decayed through the rigidity and corruption of the monarchic government.

It was the life-work of Richelieu to prevent these things. Because he did so he must be counted among the most significant statesmen of European history.

The men of the seventeenth century approached political problems still with a certain simplicity. It would have occurred to few of them to think that the wages of a French journeyman were more worthy of a statesman's study than the amours of the French King's brother. If this book seems to be—for the modern mind—a little overfull of the bickerings and intrigues of the royal family it must be remembered that such things were still of disproportionate influence in politics. The plentiful memoirs of the time, Richelieu's own letters, the reports of his agents, the despatches of ambassadors, all concentrate on personalities. Direct influence was still only in a few hands, and if the study of those men who wielded it does not give us the whole picture of an age, it gives us a very tolerable view of its political framework. The history of France during the life of Richelieu and even under the administration of Richelieu is a subject of infinite depth and complexity; yet that small part of it which is contained in the life and acts of Richelieu is a microcosm of the whole, so essentially was he of France and of his time.

Chapter 2

"Armand for the King"

DURING A TRANQUIL INTERLUDE in the religious wars, in the summer months of 1585, the last Valois King of France, Henri III, kept lustrous Court in Paris. A little apart from the iridescent favourites of the King, on the outer perimeter of the assembly, moved the Grand Provost François du Plessis sieur de Richelieu, whose task it was to enforce discipline at Court and in the town and see that the King's ordinances were carried out. He was a loyal gentleman from Poitou, of good family, small fortune and great integrity, married to Suzanne de la Porte, daughter of a substantial Parisian lawyer. This respectable pair had neither the taste nor the means to enter into the revels of the Court more fully or more often than their loyalty compelled them. They inhabited for the most part a small house on the right bank of the Seine in the parish of St. Eustache, where Suzanne was brought to bed on 9th September of her fourth child, a sickly little boy.

The baby displayed less than the usual avidity for life, refused the milk of his Parisian nurse, and, but for the skilful coaxing of a young peasant woman hurried up from Poitou, would presently have died. The question of his survival once happily settled, the parents decided to fulfil an expensive social duty by offering, on the occasion of the christening, a spectacular entertainment to the King and Court. The street from their house to the Church of St. Eustache was decorated with triumphal arches, and the elder Richelieu children, toddlers in petticoats of velvet and gold, strewed fresh roses before the distinguished guests; at the banquet afterwards a streamer over the infant's brocaded cot confronted the royal party with the motto *Regi Armandus,* "Armand for the King." Armand Jean du Plessis de Richelieu was thus officially dedicated in his cradle to the service of the Crown.

François du Plessis was thirty-seven when his third son was born. He died five years later, worn out by the exacting responsibilities of a soldier's life in time of civil war. His widow, left with five young children and heavy debts, withdrew to the family château to bring up her children under the censorious eye of her mother-in-law. The elder Madame de Richelieu reckoned the value of human beings in the quarterings of their coats of arms. Her code of conduct was strictly baronial; she had compelled her son, when he was still a young man, to jeopardise his career by killing in a duel someone against whom her noble family had a grudge, and why she had countenanced his marriage to the lawyer's daughter, Suzanne de la Porte, is unknown. Possibly a large inheritance had been expected; it had not materialised. The young widow, without even wealth to commend her, must now live as best she could with the formidable dowager. Armoured by deep religious feelings against the injuries which the haughty can inflict on the sensitive, Suzanne seems to have found happiness in the care of her family and in dutiful submission to her mother-in-law. The little that is known of this reserved, enduring woman suggests much for the character of her son; she was the source of that rigid self-command which was no part of the more tempestuous Richelieu inheritance.

The earliest years of Armand Jean du Plessis were thus spent at the château in Poitou, where the two widowed ladies lived meagrely to keep his elder brother as a page at

Court, and he learnt Latin from the chaplain and riding with the grooms. He was a delicate child, feverishly active and quick to learn. Before he was nine his career had already been decided. His eldest brother was to be a courtier; his second brother was for the Church; for him it must be the army. He was sent first to the fashionable Collège de Navarre, to master Latin grammar, composition and philosophy, and promoted thence as an adolescent to the leading military academy. Here he did all, and more than all, that the ladies in Poitou had hoped of him. He had, besides great natural talents, a zeal amounting almost to passion for hard work and phenomenal powers of memory and concentration. His gifts included a fluent and graceful speech, a well-made figure, an accurate eye, and great precision of movement. By the time he was seventeen he was an accomplished cavalier for whom all his teachers foresaw a brilliant future at Court or in the field.

At precisely this moment his elder brother, Alphonse, who was studying for the Church, startled his relatives by announcing his intention of becoming a monk. It was a blow to the family who had expected him to take orders and be appointed to the bishopric of Luçon. The bishopric, a grant from Henri III, was one of their few possessions and they relied on its revenues for a great part of their income. For some time now it had been in the hands of a nominee who wished to retire but had agreed to prolong his office for a year or two until one of the Richelieu family was ready to succeed him. The religious convictions of Alphonse could not have come upon him at a more inconvenient time for his relations. There was nothing for it but to ask—or to command—the seventeen-year-old Armand to enter the Church in his stead. The brilliant cadet must abandon his trunk-hose and close-cut velvets for an obscuring soutane, and moderate the plumed swagger of a soldier to the sober pace of an ordinand. It was much to ask of the young cavalier on the threshold of his military career.

"God's will be done," he wrote obediently to his mother, "I will accept all for the good of the Church and the glory of our house." His route was changed but not his goal. He was ambitious and he had undoubtedly seen the soldier's career as a path to high place; he must now alter his course and follow the Church to the same end. The thorough and determined way in which he made the transition from one career to the other demonstrated both the strength of his character and the consistency of his purpose.

He spoke, a little priggishly, of "the good of the Church and the glory of our house," but it is probable that even at this early age his consuming ambition was for authority and power. *"Quis erit similis mihi?"* he had chosen as the motto for a school essay: Who will be my equal? But he differed from most ambitious young men in the high seriousness of his attitude. This was evident from the moment he set out on his new career. Society in his time turned an indulgent eye on the pleasure of young men even in holy orders; and he was not expected to lead a life of austerity, to be a profound theologian or a model pastor. Many of the worldly pleasures of a young cavalier he might still furtively enjoy, if he would. As long as he avoided open scandal he would pass well enough among the bishops of his time.

Richelieu did far more than was expected of him. He withdrew at once from the social pleasures he had known and for several years ardently studied theology. He sharpened his wits on this grindstone by debating with one of the most famous dialecticians of the time, the English Jesuit, Richard Smith. At twenty-one he went to Rome, where his learning and good manners made an excellent impression at the Vatican, and in Rome, while he was still several years under the canonical age, he was consecrated Bishop of Luçon.

A difficult decision now lay before him. It was open to him, with a popular elder brother already at Court and the reputation of a good preacher, to hover about the halls of the Louvre, courting the royal attention, and hoping for some official appointment. The alternative was to be Bishop of Luçon in sober earnest. Of his own will he chose this latter course, and buried himself for several years in a wretched country town among the insalubrious marshes of the West. One of his reasons was his own and his family's poverty, but his exemplary conduct when he reached his see shows that he had another design in what he did. He knew no better way to learn the business of administration than by this first-hand experience.

In the heart of winter, a few days before Christmas 1608, Richelieu took possession of his office. The chapter, who resented the privileges of his family, welcomed him coolly, and the leading townsfolk, many of whom were Huguenots, met him with mingled curiosity and resentment. In answer to their words of official welcome the young bishop was friendly but cautious. "I know that there are some of this company who are not one with us in Faith," he said, "but I hope that we shall be one in love, and I shall do all in my power to make it so, for that will be best for us and most pleasing to the King, whom we must strive to serve in all things." Thus at the outset of his official career he emphasised the duty of subjects to their King, the recurrent theme of his political theory.

It was dismal and damp at Luçon. Every chimney in the episcopal palace smoked so badly that no fire could be lit; the building was filthy and ruinous and when the young bishop unpacked his small belongings he found that some of his vestments had been stolen on the journey. The cathedral was decayed, the dirty little town stank of marsh-fever, and there was not so much as a garden or avenue anywhere in which he could take a quiet walk. "My house is my prison," he wrote to a friend, and at once busied himself setting things to rights. He sent for a new set of vestments, ordered two dozen silver dinner-plates from Paris, and a fur muff to keep his hands warm. He engaged a competent major-domo—so competent that he stayed in his service for life—and wrote to the authorities pleading that Luçon was assessed for taxation at far too high a rate.

Experience was to sharpen Richelieu's judgment, learning was to enlarge his understanding, but even in these early years, his dominating preoccupations are already clear. Thus he believed in building up immediately the fallen prestige of the bishop by having his house properly organised and his table furnished with silver. Throughout his life he insisted—not without justification in the epoch in which he lived—that manners, formalities and the outward appearance of a seemly, but not ostentatious, wealth were important for those in authority; again, in taking steps to relieve the burden of taxes on his flock, he showed the practical and responsible attitude towards immediate problems which always characterised his policy. Last of all, when he ordered a muff for his chilblained hands he was thinking of preserving the maximum efficiency in an unhealthy body, which threatened, throughout his life, to hamper his vigorous mind. In spite of his military training and muscular agility, Richelieu had never acquired any solid health. His youthful troubles were bad circulation, bad digestion and recurrent, prostrating attacks of migraine. If he fussed a little unduly about his health for a young man he was wise to do so. Only by continuous attention to it was he, later, to be able to keep alive at all.

Ill-health was never for Richelieu an excuse for inactivity. The few letters that have survived from this period of his life give a composite picture of the many preoccupations of his mind. He was concerned for the welfare of his flock and the dignity of his position, for good order throughout the diocese, for religious education and the salvation of souls. He travelled, in all weathers, to visit his outlying parishes; he drew up a simple catechism for the instruction of the ignorant, and he corresponded with such great figures of the French religious renaissance as Father Bérulle in Paris, and the noble Antoinette d'Orléans, who had become an exemplary nun at the neighbouring convent of Fontevrault, and who was later to found her own order, the Daughters of Calvary.

After the religious conflicts and disasters of the past century, France was in the midst of that religious revival to which St. Francis de Sales and St. Vincent de Paul contributed the parallel forces of mystical and practical Christianity. Reform, and a new spirit of austere devotion, was blowing a cold invigorating gale through the convents and monasteries of France. At about the same time as Richelieu, for family reasons, turned from the army to the Church, Jacqueline Arnauld, known in religion as Mère Angélique, had been made abbess of the great convent of Port Royal by her worldly relations to secure the revenues of the convent to her family. It was no great deprivation for a young girl; she was expected to lead a social life, and so, until her nineteenth year, she did. But on a September day in 1609 her father and mother rode out from Paris to Port Royal with a cavalcade of cheerful friends, in vain. The doors were closed. Their daughter spoke to them only through a grille; henceforth, she said, she would abide by her vows. The struggle between obedience to her Heavenly and her earthly father was overpowering and as her indignant family withdrew she fainted away at her post. It was the beginning of the whole great movement of reform connected with the name of Port Royal.

Such ardours and fervours in a lesser degree were common all over France. Peasant girls had visions and received the stigmata; fashionable young people formed congregations devoted to the Virgin and vied with each other in austerity, prayer and works. New convents and new orders were founded; the Carmelites of St. Theresa reached France from Spain in 1604, and the reformed Franciscans, the Capuchins, attracted recruits from the noblest families; they had attracted Richelieu's brother Alphonse. With the new spirit of devotion went the determination to win back the heretics. While Huguenot fervour had cooled to a grey ash of its former self, the young Catholics glowed to make converts.

Luçon, in the heart of Poitou, was in a land much infected with the Huguenot heresy. All the greater were the efforts of the reformed Catholic Church to win it back. The Capuchins preached and worked indefatigably among the people. The most eminent of the French Capuchins was

François le Clerc du Tremblay, called in religion Father Joseph, a highly educated man of good family, and only a few years older than Richelieu. The moving spirit of the serious and intelligent French who had founded the Oratory in Paris to train priests in the ways of preaching, teaching and self-abnegation in priesthood was Father Bérulle. The young Bishop of Luçon knew and revered both these men, and both knew him. Bérulle founded his second Oratory for young priests in Luçon during the years of Richelieu's episcopate. But it was Father Joseph who, meeting him first through the intervention of the saintly Antoinette d'Orléans, soon made him the confidant of the great mission which he believed must be undertaken by Catholic Christendom against the heretic and the infidel. Father Joseph's ambition was to set on foot a new crusade against the Turk.

Neither Father Bérulle nor Father Joseph can have imagined Richelieu to be a man of his own kind. Indeed his value to the causes in which they believed lay precisely in those more worldly characteristics which he possessed. He was a conscientious bishop and a devout believer, but his ability and his ambition also might be valuable to the faith. They were not alone among the devout men of France's religious renaissance to single out the Bishop of Luçon as one of God's possible instruments for the achievement of the necessary things of this world. It is difficult to estimate the problems of Richelieu's later career without understanding how deeply his outlook and policy were governed by a genuine religious conviction, and how much the devout party in France came to count on him during the years before he rose to power.

Richelieu was a cautious, calculating and a very ambitious man, but he sought power for himself with the good of the Church and of the French monarchy in mind, and later he sought the greatness of the French monarchy so that it might serve and save the Church. It is possible to accuse Richelieu in all this of fatal misconceptions as to Christian doctrine, or indeed of an entire self-deception.

But we shall understand neither him nor his epoch if we doubt the sincerity of the religious convictions which went on equal footing with his personal ambition.

The young bishop's calculating eye was still fixed on Paris. In 1610 the King, Henri IV, was murdered by the Spanish-paid Ravaillac as he was setting out to war with Spain. Richelieu at once composed a letter of flattering condolence to the widowed Queen-Regent Marie de Medici. His friends dissuaded him from presenting it; it was, they pointed out, a little too obvious. He waited, impatiently, for another five years. By 1615 he was well enough known to be selected by the clergy to compose the address to the throne from the Estates General—the representative body of the French nation—which was called in that year. The address, a loyal and courtly piece of work, included a survey of current political problems of remarkable breadth, detail and judgment. Its chief interest today lies, however, in the significant passage in which the Bishop of Luçon draws the royal attention to the peculiar fitness of the clergy for positions of trust in the state.

Their calling, he argued, was of great avail to make them apt for such offices, for it obliged them to acquire knowledge, to be honourable and to govern themselves with prudence. These, he continued, were the chief qualities needed in those who were to serve the state. The clergy were also more free than other men of those private interests which so often wrong the common weal, for, since they might not marry, they had no need to amass wealth on earth, but were compelled, even when serving their King and country, to think of nothing except an eternal and glorious reward in Heaven above.

The broad hint was taken and the Queen-mother began to make use of the Bishop of Luçon in the complex internal diplomacy of France. He was sent, for instance, to pacify the young King's rebellious cousin, the Prince de Condé, and a few months later he was appointed ambassador to Spain. This latter mission came to nothing for, in November

1616 on the eve of his departure for Madrid, he was called to a place on the Council of State itself as the minister responsible for Foreign Affairs.

So far there was little to prove, except to those who knew him well, that the Bishop of Luçon was anything more than a nimble-witted place hunter with a talent for oratory and organisation and a refreshingly high sense of his duties to the public and to the Almighty. His first brief tenure of office revealed the strength and independence of his judgment.

He had risen as the nominee and favourite of the Queen-mother whose favour he retained by a careful expenditure of the erotic flattery to which the foolish, fading woman was amenable. Ever since her husband's death, Marie de Medici had adopted a policy of appeasement towards Spain. Her plans had been crowned in 1615 by the cere-monious exchange of royal brides on the Pyrenaean frontier. Madame Elisabeth, eldest daughter of France, had been given to the Infante Don Philip of Spain, and the Infanta Anna, eldest daughter of Spain, had been received in return by the boy King of France.

This double marriage represented the acquiescence of the French monarchy in the King of Spain's domination of Europe. France, which, under the vigorous rule of Henri IV, had been the defender of the smaller nations against this puissant aggression, had been reduced to the part of a satellite. Marie de Medici was not wholly to blame. The minority of a King in a country still divided by religious conflict and by the sectional ambitions of the nobles was not a favourable, or even a possible, time for challenging a powerful neighbour. Peace was necessary and the Queen-mother had bought it for the price at which Spain would sell. Besides, the political spokesmen of France's Catholic revival, the large party known as *les dévots,* were behind the Regent's policy. The Spanish monarchy was the cru-sading power which was striving to reorganise Europe once again as united Catholic Christendom. In this crusade, where should Catholic France stand if not at the side of

Spain? So at least the devout party in France usually argued at this time. The Queen-mother had followed the tide.

Richelieu would not have been appointed Foreign Minister had he not appeared in sympathy with this point of view. Indeed as a Churchman and a personal friend of such men as Father Joseph, Father Bérulle and the King's own Jesuit confessor, Father Arnoux, he must have seen much to commend a policy which bound the two great Catholic powers together, even at the expense of French prestige. Both as a good Catholic and as a practical statesman he could not oppose it. Continual threats of internal revolt from the discontented nobility forced the French government to seek above all safety and stability, and the time had not yet come to reverse a foreign policy which at least secured peace on the frontiers.

But Richelieu had not even at this date any abiding faith in the policy of appeasement. He suspected, with cynical sagacity, that the Spanish crusade for a reunited Christendom was not disinterested but tended rather to the aggrandisement of the Spanish monarchy than the rescue of the Catholic Church. He was already anxiously aware that the French government had gone too far on the path of conciliation and that Spanish power must be challenged before it became so great that challenge was impossible. In his view the only constructive long-term policy for his country was to solicit and hold the alliances of all those lesser powers of Europe which feared the aggression of Spain. He made a first step in this direction by circularising the Protestant princes of Europe with the gratuitous but reassuring information that the Franco-Spanish alliance must not be regarded as in any way a menace to France's other friendships.

This cautious counter-move against Spanish domination was an interesting indication of Richelieu's point of view but he was prevented from moving any further in that direction by the sudden collapse of the government. His first tenure of power was brief and its consequences were bitter.

Louis XIII was sixteen years old. His majority had been

proclaimed some years earlier, but his mother and her favourites continued to govern France. Her favourites were her foster-sister, the Italian adventuress, Leonora Galigai, and her husband, Concini, a pair of vulgar profiteers who ruled Court and state by the complaisance of the Queen-mother. Concini carried his honours with a high hand, swaggered it out with the nobles and openly despised the King. Louis, a sulky, undergrown adolescent, opened his rancorous heart to his only friend, his Master of the Horse, the ingratiating Provençal, Luynes. It was not from these two, a morose child and an empty-headed sportsman, that Concini anticipated trouble. He reckoned without the hatred stored up among the French nobility and the Parisian populace. A man without a friend is an easy prey. His wife, more apprehensive, had already suggested that it was time for them to withdraw to Florence with their plunder. Concini would not be warned of the conspiracy fast growing against him. On 24th April, 1617, the Baron de Vitry, Captain of the King's Guard, on orders from Luynes, shot Concini dead as he entered the Louvre. Among the fifty gentlemen-at-arms who formed his life guard and his train only one drew sword in his defence. His wife, characteristically wearing a number of the Crown jewels, was arrested within the hour. Throughout the palace there was an uproar of "Vive le Roi" and young Louis scrambled on to a billiard table and from this unorthodox perch joyfully received the acclamations of his courtiers. "I am King now," he repeated, "I am your King."

The Queen-mother was a prisoner in her apartments; her ministry was dissolved and one at least of Richelieu's colleagues was hurried to the Bastille. He himself had insured against total disaster by cultivating Luynes, so that when he made a cautious appearance among the cheering throng round the billiard table, he was greeted with tolerance if not with enthusiasm.

The danger was not over. Next day, as he crossed the Pont Neuf in his coach, it stuck in a crowd of angry citizens; too late to turn back, the Bishop of Luçon saw with

dismay that the mob had got hold of Concini's body from
the neighbouring church and were tearing it to pieces. At
that moment one of his coach horses almost knocked down
a man in the crowd. They surged angrily round him. Should
they recognise him as one of Concini's ministers he knew
that he was lost. He believed, however, that his face would
not be known to them; boldly he leaned from the coach
and asked them what they were doing. They told him. He
nodded approval: "What loyalty to the King," he exclaimed, and suggested that they should all shout "Vive le
Roi" while he led the cheers. They cheered the King in
unison, and Richelieu's coach trundled safely on, past the
unseemly remains of his late patron.

In confronting the King and in confronting the mob
Richelieu showed great presence of mind and great callous-
ness. Both aspects of his character are typical: his life and
his career were sacred to him because he felt both to be
sacred to France. Concini had never been anything but a
means to an end. Gratitude to the dead at such a moment
would have been out of place. For Richelieu the future was
all-important. Yet he was not wholly forgetful of the man
who had raised him first to power. He left in his memoirs
a portrait of Concini which is generous both to his character and his talent. Moreover when he came to power he
appointed as captain of his guard, Monsieur de St. Georges,
the only man of Concini's life-guard who had tried to help
his master.

Meanwhile he was still in the service of the Queen-
mother; in this capacity he arranged for her withdrawal to
Blois, whence he took care to inform the King and Luynes
of all her movements. The manœuvre did not soften either
of their hearts. For several years yet he was to remain, in
the King's opinion, an ambitious and time-serving man who
was suspect for having been a protégé of Concini. It was
reward enough to leave him unpunished. As soon as Richelieu understood that his part of self-appointed spy would
profit him nothing, he esteemed it best for his career to
dissociate himself altogether from the exiled Marie de

Medici and to strive rather to climb back into favour by his own merits. For the time being he went back to Luçon.

While he devoted himself once again to his episcopal duties the realm of France continued as sickly under the new régime as under the old. Luynes had been clever enough to take advantage of the King's adolescent affection but he was not clever enough to know when to cease taking advantage of it. By the time he died in 1621 his credit with Louis was long exhausted. The affairs of France, meanwhile, were feebly guided by the surviving ministers of Henri IV, recalled from retirement by the inexperienced King. These vacillating, captious old men, corrupt with envy and intrigue, bungled the country's policy at home and abroad. Puisieux de Sillery, La Vieuville—their names mean nothing to France or to history. During their time the finances of the government grew progressively more entangled while Spain consolidated a formidable position in Europe, and the lesser powers, which had once looked to the King of France, ceased to believe in the possibility of a French revival. The Elector of Saxony put a French envoy out of countenance by asking whether there was any such person as the King of France.

For seven years, from 1617-1624, Richelieu pursued his frustrated way in the wilderness. Once, through the jealousy of Luynes, he was exiled for a year to Avignon. He had indeed a very low opinion of the favourite who made use of his power to enrich his rapacious family, starting with his two brothers and working steadily through to his remotest cousins. "If France were all for sale," wrote Richelieu, "they would buy France from France itself." The Queen-mother, meanwhile, made herself the focus of aristocratic discontent, and to prevent or assuage revolt Luynes himself had to have recourse to Richelieu. Twice over the insinuating Bishop of Luçon persuaded Marie de Medici to make an accommodation with her son and so rob the malcontent nobility of a leader for their revolt.

When the last of these agreements was signed at Angoulême in August 1620, Richelieu hoped that, for reward, he would be appointed at least to the Royal Council. The King preferred to recompense him by applying to the Pope to make him a Cardinal and even for this he had to wait nearly two years.

The frustration was exasperating, all the more now that his ambition and his abilities were both well known. The papal nuncio declared frankly that the Bishop of Luçon was a great enough man to rule both the King and his mother. In fact the animosity felt towards him by the King's other ministers seems to have been the measure of their respect for his ability; they feared that if he once became one of them he would completely dominate them. All this while Richelieu watched with dismay the clumsy misman-agement of France's affairs in the interests of Spain, and strove by every indirect means in his power to change the course of events. He profited by the reconciliation between the King and his mother to win Marie de Medici to his point of view so that she should present his opinions to the King as her own. He inspired the popular pamphleteer, Fancan, in a leaflet called *La France Mourante,* to make propaganda among the people.

In the meantime changes had taken place among the ranks of the French devout. Father Joseph had been for some years seriously concerned with a plan for a Crusade against the Turk in which all Europe was to join. The ro-mantic Duke of Nevers was to lead it; he had founded a new fighting order called the Christian Militia for the pur-pose, and had already received appeals for help from the Greeks, the Albanians and the Poles. The Duke had ap-proached the Pope, the Grand Duke of Tuscany and the German princes with his plans. By 1618 he was raising troops in earnest and had ordered ships for the enterprise, while Father Joseph preached the Holy War up and down the land like a new Peter the Hermit. Then, unexpectedly, the King of Spain refused permission for the Christian Militia to recruit in his dominons and the defection of Spain, the greatest Catholic power of Europe, was the death-blow to the Crusade.

The event had a powerful effect on the opinions of Father Joseph. He perceived that the reuniting of Europe was an essential first step in the direction of a Holy War, and that the pretensions of Spain to act as the unifying power in the name of the Catholic Church were false. Spain had betrayed his Crusade; he could not forgive this crime. From now on, all his hopes were concentrated on the resurgence of his native France, and on the assumption by France of the leadership of Christendom. For that great work, Richelieu seemed the most apt instrument.

The power of this fanatic, whose cadaverous face, red beard, broken sandals and ragged gown were familiar at most of the Courts of Europe, was considerable. He was sent on diplomatic missions, he was the repository of state secrets, and the trusted adviser of Kings and their ministers. His influence was now fiercely applied to getting Richelieu appointed to the Royal Council.

Thus, at last, in the spring of 1624 the King yielded to his mother's request and Father Joseph's persuasion. The first minister, La Vieuville, fought hard against the appointment. He suggested that an outer cabinet should be formed in which Richelieu could sit without coming into immediate contact with the King; Richelieu refused the trap, for he perceived that it was intended merely to prevent his access to the sovereign. La Vieuville tried to send him on an embassy; Richelieu declined the honour. He knew that the weight of his ability and of his friends' persuasion must bear down the tottering opposition at last. Sure enough, late in April, the King sent for the Cardinal and offered him a seat on the Council. He wrote at once to the Capuchin: "Since you are the chief agent whom God has used to lead me to those honours to which I am now raised, I hold myself bound to inform you before all others that it has pleased the King to give me the position of his first minister."

Yet Richelieu was speaking a little before the event, for the decrepit La Vieuville was still nominally at the head of the government. From April to August the unequal conflict between them lasted. Richelieu first sustained a claim to take precedence of all the King's other ministers on account of his rank as a Cardinal. This point gained, to the discomfiture of La Vieuville, he next inspired the journalist Fancan to attack the first minister in a pamphlet called *La Voix Publique au Roi*. La Vieuville was accused of rapacity and corruption which surpassed that of Concini and Luynes. The facts were a little exaggerated, but there was much substantial truth in them. La Vieuville had moreover displayed that casual contempt of his King, which the unhappy Louis seemed fated to inspire, by giving instructions to ambassadors in terms quite different from those approved at the Royal Council. Richelieu was not slow to bring this to the royal notice.

La Vieuville was arrested on 13th August, 1624, and on 24th August Richelieu was appointed head of the Royal Council. It was a few days short of his thirty-ninth birthday. During the two-thirds of his life which had already elapsed France had been distracted by religious war, and united by the great and popular Henri IV only to fall into decay once more during the first fourteen years of his son's reign. Richelieu was to use the third part of his life still left to him to restore the threatened monarchy, to reintegrate the disordered nation, and to establish the solid foundation of French leadership in Europe, whether in the arts of peace or by the power of war.

Chapter 3

The Situation in 1624

THE ASSOCIATION of Cardinal Richelieu with Louis XIII decided not only the future of France, but the future of Western Europe. It is therefore reasonable to pause in the unfolding of the story to consider the state of Europe, the state of France and the character of the two men whose co-operation for the next eighteen years was to have such wide effects.

The religious question, Catholic against Protestant, Reformation against Counter-reformation, still appeared to dominate European politics in 1624. Over a century after the rugged Luther had started in Germany that great breakaway from the body of united Christendom, the quarrel between the conflicting doctrines was still unassuaged. It had been complicated further by the rise of Calvinism on the Protestant side of the barrier; this was a more acid and energetic creed than that of Luther, organised rigidly for survival and combat, which from its original stronghold, the independent republic of Geneva, had gradually penetrated the whole of northern Europe. The struggle had been intensified on the Catholic side by the appearance of the organised proselytising orders of the Jesuits and Capuchins. At the same time the political contours of the quarrel had been sharply modified by the rise to European domination, during the sixteenth century, of the militant Catholic Spanish monarchy.

The Spanish kingdoms had become united at the close of the Middle Ages as a crusading power. The Crusade against the Moorish power in the Spanish Peninsula itself had ended with the fall of Granada in 1492; but the militant spirit lived on and only a generation later found an outlet against the heresies within Christendom itself. By 1624 the religious conflict in Europe had thus assumed a somewhat confusing shape. There was general civil war in Germany because the Protestant Bohemians had revolted against their Catholic King Ferdinand II and called in a German Calvinist prince from the Rhineland, Frederick V of the Palatinate, to their rescue. Frederick had been defeated and Bohemia ruthlessly restored to the Church. But his cause had been taken up by the Calvinist Dutch, who were themselves involved in a war with Catholic Spain from whose suzerainty they had revolted sixty years before, and against whom they had been fighting, with one interval, ever since. The Spaniards carried out operations against the Dutch from the Catholic southern provinces of the Low Countries (which we today call Belgium) and from vantage points on the Rhine seized from the defeated Frederick V. It was natural, therefore, for the Dutch to give hospitality to the refugee Frederick and his family and to strive in their own interests to dislodge the Spaniards from his land. This was not, however, the end of the story. The rightful and victorious King of Bohemia, Ferdinand of Habsburg, had been elected Holy Roman Emperor, as the suzerain of Germany was called; encouraged by his success in Bohemia, he had set out to destroy the power of Protestantism in Germany and if possible to restore to the Church all that it had lost during the last century. The King of England was the father-in-law of the dispossessed Frederick, the King of Denmark was his uncle, and both were Protestants. Neither had as yet declared war on the Emperor, but both were expected to do so at any moment.

Yet religion was not the only motive force in this confused conflict. It was probably no longer even the strongest. Violent as those passions seemed they were only the exhalations which concealed the true outline of European politics. The fundamental division of Europe was not religious but political. The contest, in the final resort, was not one of Church against Church but of nation against nation.

This word *nation* expresses what is to us a familiar idea of the state; but 300 years ago nation-states were only at the beginning of their existence. A sense of solidarity existed already among people who spoke the same language, or lived under the same government. This could be exploited and intensified by clever political leadership, such, for instance, as that of Queen Elizabeth in England, or of Henri IV in France. But national solidarity was rarely so well developed as to withstand, in the absence of such leadership, the disintegrating pull of other forces. The French people, before the accession of Henri IV, had not only been divided among themselves by differences of religion and interest, but had thought it the most natural thing in the world to call in foreigners to their help. Thus the French Catholics had called in the Spaniards to fight for them, and the Huguenots or Protestants had called in the Germans. In Germany, while there was much sentimental devotion to the Germanic liberties and the Germanic idea, there was nothing to hold together the many states of the so-called Holy Roman Empire except a common language. This force was quite inadequate against the sectional interests of local groups and regional princes, and Germany presented a lamentable picture of warring egoistical states.

Thus although the term *nation* existed, and although some nation-states—England, Denmark, Sweden, Spain—were already recognisable entities, the modern conception of the nation with all its sentimental and political force, had hardly yet developed. Older loyalties contended perpetually with the comparatively new idea of loyalty to the nation: loyalty to rank, or religion, even to the orders of chivalry. Thus the great nobles of Europe made personal alliances with each other regardless of the policy of their King. French dukes married Italian princesses, German princes married the heiresses of French noble houses, often without the approval of their respective overlords. Some of them held lands under the suzerainty of several different princes. The Duke of Lorraine, a prince of the Holy Roman Empire, held most of his duchy from the Emperor, but fragments of the frontiers were under the French King. Another border dukedom, that of Bouillon with its fortress capital at Sedan, a strategic place on the French frontier, was technically a part of the Holy Roman Empire though the Duke of Bouillon possessed lands under the French crown as well and ranked as one of France's great nobles. The religious Duke of Nevers, that powerful French nobleman, whose crusading zeal the Greeks and Albanians had called in aid against the Turks, came of an Italian family and was heir to the Italian dukedom of Mantua.

The orders and honours bestowed by monarchs were not, as they are today, gracious tokens of official gratitude. They still carried, or could be made to carry, some of the feudal obligations of the old orders of chivalry. When Sir Thomas Arundell of Wardour, while travelling abroad, accepted a title from the Emperor, Queen Elizabeth sent him to the Tower with the caustic rebuke that she would not have her dogs wearing other men's collars. The phrase is more than a typical example of the Queen's wit; it expresses the truth of the situation. Elizabeth knew the danger of having a subject of hers under an obligation to a foreign prince. One of Richelieu's most frequent troubles was that the French nobility were, as far as their King was concerned, frequently dogs wearing other men's collars—and coming when other men whistled. They entered into intrigues with the Emperor or the King of Spain and regarded it as their right to do so. The idea that such conduct was treason to the *nation* never occurred to them.

Yet it was precisely these men who, when Richelieu came to power, still controlled many of the most important offices in the kingdom. The great provincial governorships, the highest commands in the army, the admiralship of the French coasts—these were the vital positions occupied by men whose code of honour and sense of duty belonged stubbornly to a prenational age. French politics for the first half of the seventeenth century are riddled with their treacheries—although it is unjust to characterise by the term of treachery acts which were anachronistic rather than treasonous.

Yet in spite of these survivals from a differently constituted feudal Europe, public opinion among the now prosperous and vocal middle classes had already gone far towards establishing the idea that the nation, the homeland, was something for whose greatness and power it was right and honourable to work. Patriotism in its worst and its best senses was coming into being; Richelieu knew well how to develop the nascent patriotism which he found in France, and although for him the feeling was more closely associated with the idea of the King than of the nation, he too shared in the growing popular sentiment.

If the nation was still an imperfect political concept there was above or alongside it an aged institution of the greatest importance—dynastic monarchy. It was indeed by modernising this institution that Richelieu was to give concrete shape to the French nation. Monarchy, as practised in Western Europe at this time and for some centuries past, meant the domination of a single important family in each country. Where such a family was strong and the inheritance passed without dispute from one member to the next the development of national solidarity tended to progress smoothly. But in countries where the effective power of the Crown was weakened by a disputed succession or by a dynasty not strong enough to maintain itself against rivals, national development was less sure.

Of the great ruling families in Europe two stood out above the rest: the Habsburg dynasty who ruled in Spain, Austria, parts of Italy and part of the Netherlands; and the

Bourbon dynasty who ruled in France. The political fissure which divided Europe was the dynastic feud between the ruling families of France and Spain.

There seems to be a tendency throughout the history of Western Europe since the collapse of Rome for one power to strive always towards the domination of the others. In the earlier Middle Ages this power had been the so-called Holy Roman Empire of the German nation, based on the Rhineland and South Germany; its chief opponent had been the French monarchy. With the disintegration of the Empire into a cluster of quarrelling states, the centre of the quarrel had shifted and from the later fifteenth century onwards it had become a struggle between the ruling dynasties of France and Spain.

At the Reformation the dynastic quarrel had briefly gone underground when the most Christian King of France and the Catholic King of Spain—for these were their respective titles—had felt the necessity for taking common action against heresy. But the united front of the Catholic powers had never lasted long.

Thus, for instance, Catherine de Medici had taken up the cause of the Dutch rebels, and the French monarchy under Henri IV had played with *éclat* the part of defender of European liberties against the aggression of Spain. With his murder in 1610 this defiance had given place once more to cautious appeasement.

The policy was not wise. French territory was bounded on every landward side by that of the Habsburg dynasty. The King of Spain, who ruled also in the kingdom of Naples, the Duchy of Milan and the Belgic provinces, was the head of a prolific and united breed of princes. His uncle (who was also his cousin) was that King Ferdinand of Bohemia, Archduke of Styria and Holy Roman Emperor, whose religious policy had precipitated the revolt in Bohemia and was now prolonging the war in Germany. Cousins reigned in Tyrol and Tuscany and an uncle by marriage in Savoy. Genoa was almost a tributary power.

The main political projects of the Habsburg rulers

formed a remarkable unity. The kingdom of Spain had been engaged for the last sixty years in the struggle to regain the rebellious northern provinces of the Netherlands. The possession of these provinces, which had formed themselves into an independent Protestant power in the last century under the Prince of Orange, William the Silent, was essential to the welfare of the Spanish Crown. They were an important source of revenue, and they commanded the Narrow Seas whence the growing maritime power of England could be checked. Military operations against the Dutch were carried on from the loyal southern provinces of the Netherlands; the troops needed for these operations were for the most part recruited in the Spanish-controlled provinces of northern Italy and transported to the Low Countries across the Alps and down the Rhine. A Genoese general, Spinola, held the high command. The line of communication from North Italy, along the Val Telline, over the Alps and down the Rhine to the Netherlands was nothing less than the spinal cord of the Austro-Spanish Empire. Through the Emperor Ferdinand's control of Germany and more especially of the Rhine provinces, the King of Spain saw his way to the defeat of the Dutch.

The increasing pressure on the Dutch was also a threat to the French who, with a powerful Habsburg Germany to the east, as well as a powerful Habsburg Spain to the south, were in danger of encirclement. Such formidable neighbours were bound sooner or later to assert an interfering authority within France itself, which might not end until they had completely absorbed the Bourbon dynasty into their own and the French kingdom with it.

This was the situation when Richelieu came to power. It was a situation whose development he himself had watched for the last seven years with growing anxiety. In his view a total reversal of policy could alone rescue France. The balance of power in Europe must be restored and tilted once again in France's favour by organising the scattered and dispirited opponents of Spain.

But could France redeem the position? Geographically

the land frontiers were vulnerable and the long sea-coast, with no navy to protect it, was merely a source of weakness. Politically, the state of the country was deplorable. The independent power of the nobility made it nearly impossible for the King to carry out any policy of which they disapproved. The Huguenot minority had been given, by the Edict of Nantes, the control of several important fortresses and the right not only to practice their religion, but also to establish their own law courts, to exclude Catholics from their cities and, in fact, to constitute themselves as a small autonomous state within the state. Their effective leader, Henri, Duke of Rohan, was moreover one of the greatest nobles of France so that he combined in his person the two dangerous characteristics of being a dissident in religion and almost a prince in his own right. It was thus possible that the whole dangerous Huguenot enclave might be involved in a revolt of the nobles, or conversely, that the great nobles might band together with one of their number if the Huguenots should decide to make trouble. This linking of the Huguenot interest with that of the nobility had been a dangerous feature in the civil wars of the last century.

The royal authority was very loosely established throughout the country. In the later Middle Ages French Kings had sought to strengthen their power against the great nobles by seeking the alliance of lesser nobility, merchants and lawyers. They had bought their friendships with concessions of petty authority or local privilege, by which in turn the lesser men had become great. These creatures of the monarchy were now in their turn beginning to stand on their rights against the Crown. In France the situation was doubly serious because the older problem of the great nobles had never been solved, and thus the second group of hostile forces had come into being, while the first was still active.

As in England—where the House of Commons had become critical of the royal authority and increasingly obstructive—so in France the six regional assemblies, or

Parlements, with Paris at their head, were also critical and obstructive. These bodies differed in several ways from the English Parliament. They were not elective, they were regional, not national, and they had no control over taxation. They consisted chiefly of lawyers and their function was to register and authorise the laws made by the King and his Council, and subsequently to defend them against infringement. They were in fact Courts of Appeal with special legislative functions. Their criticism, modifications, and even rejections of the royal decrees had been very marked since the close of the last century, and it had been the policy of the government to accept these attacks with as good a grace as possible. It was necessary for the King to have the *noblesse de robe,* the local families of lawyers and officials from whom the *Parlements* were recruited, on his side if he could, for on them depended the maintenance of the royal power in the provinces.

Threatened by the power of the great nobles and compelled to pacify a captious official class, the French monarchy was also without any stable financial support. Its revenues were derived chiefly from the two great taxes, the *taille,* or poll-tax, and the *gabelle,* the tax on salt. But the taxes were farmed out and those who had the administering of them partook generously of the proceeds. Moreover, they assessed their friends, or those who bribed them most freely, at very low rates, so that the wealthy paid less and the poor more than was their due. When the money at length reached the royal treasury it fell among thieves once again. There was no organisation, no effective system of accounts. Luynes, Sillery, La Vieuville had all helped themselves freely. Meanwhile the King was deep in debt and all the curtains in the Louvre were in rags.

There was, however, another side to this picture. The animosity of the nobles to the bourgeoisie and of the bourgeoisie to the nobles made a *united* opposition against the King unlikely. The *Etats Generaux,* the Estates General, which was the elected assembly of the kingdom called to vote for exceptional subsidies, might be critical, but the three Estates (nobles, clergy, smaller gentry) were just as likely to fall foul of each other. In 1615 there had been a clamorous disagreement between the nobility and the gentry because a nobleman had impetuously killed one of their number in a duel, whereupon the Third Estate took it upon themselves to condemn the nobleman to death, an action which the First Estate said, haughtily, was a breach of privilege.

It would thus be possible for an astute man to divide and conquer the critics of the French monarchy, and for a strong man to profit by the very corruption of the administrative and financial system to dominate and recreate it. Something of these possibilities had been seen under the administration of the strong and popular Henri IV. But the ground gained had been mostly lost during the fourteen years since his death. All had now to be begun again.

Thus when Richelieu was called to the right hand of Louis XIII the problem before him was twofold. He had to challenge the power of Spain and he had to create in France the conditions necessary to make that challenge effective. The problem was formidable enough to appal the most far-seeing statesman. Richelieu was not appalled. He knew that he had the ability and only feared that he might lack the physical stamina. He needed, however, something more than great ability and physical endurance to ensure his success. He needed the intelligent co-operation of the King; without this he could have done nothing.

Legend has sometimes represented Louis XIII as a helpless, hypnotised puppet in the control of his tremendous minister. The King's reserved nature, feeble health and many eccentricities gave some ground for the growth of this fable. But it is a fable. A sickly, strong-willed and over-imaginative child, Louis had responded badly to a bad education. His father had been cheerfully confident in the efficacy of the rod; his mother boxed his ears when she lost her temper but relied more regularly on emotional blackmail. (It remained her strongest political weapon for many years.) Between them and the riotous atmosphere of the royal nursery, where the King's legitimate and illegitimate brood scrambled up together. Louis was a maladjusted child when he succeeded to the throne at the age of nine. After that came the additional complication of accepting in theory his exalted position as King while he remained in fact the unloved and unattractive object of his mother's and her favourites' sneers. He grew up a resentful neurotic. His genuine religious feeling did not serve to control his impulses towards violence and petty cruelty. Thus his passion for the chase was merciless and he sometimes rode his horses to death; he kept small birds flying about his rooms at the Louvre, tamed and fed them himself, only, in the end, to let loose a hawk among them so that he might watch the twittering victims in frantic flight among the mirrors and chandeliers.

He would have been affectionate had he been allowed to show it; he was intelligent, but without the energy to give it expression. His education had filled him with spiteful obsessions against those whom he believed had hurt or humiliated him. Suspicious even of his most devoted friends, proud, secretive, rather mean and usually ungracious, he yearned for the human affection that he was temperamentally unable to inspire and from time to time became involved in obsessive emotional friendships. His marriage had proved a disaster. A plain and placid woman might have soothed him, an affectionate woman might have released his frustrated tenderness. Anne of Austria was beautiful, self-willed and demanding. Her frank pink-and-white allurements were altogether too startling a challenge for this nervous, immature young man. The lovely, neglected Queen became a permanent embarrassment. Once she had been pregnant, she had miscarried, typically, because she had been romping with her maids of honour. Louis dismissed the maids of honour but the Queen conceived no second child.

Yet with all his shortcomings Louis had three outstanding qualities. He was personally brave; he had the perspicacity to recognise in Richelieu an outstanding intellect and to give him wholehearted support; and he had a vision of his duty as a sovereign which enabled him in a crisis to rise above himself, to stifle alike his personal resentments and his ill-judged affections.

These virtues are not to be despised. James I of England was a far more able man than Louis XIII, but James could not have sacrificed a favourite to the good of the kingdom, as Louis was one day to sacrifice his favourite Cinq Mars. Charles I of England was the equal of Louis in intelligence and his superior in most other ways, but he kept back every able minister he had because, unlike Louis, he could not endure a position in which the minister appeared to be a greater man than the King. Neither of these Kings, nor perhaps any other prince in Europe at this time, would have submitted so willingly to the parental advice and lecturing which Richelieu, in one vast and valuable memorandum after another, bestowed throughout the years on the King of France. The self-effacement of Louis XIII must be counted as not the least of the causes which contributed to the consolidation of the French state, for the achievement of the Cardinal was made possible only by the conduct of the King. There is a certain dignified gratitude expressed by Richelieu in a significant phrase in his *Political Testament*. "The capacity to permit his ministers to serve him is not the least of qualities in a great King." There are moreover signs of a genuine affection in the notes which the King sometimes wrote on the Cardinal's memoranda. Thus more than once he expresses relief and pleasure to hear that his minister is in good health and once even ends a letter with the quaint attractive signature *Louis de très bon cœur*—"Louis, with all my heart."

The character of Richelieu was already well enough known to Louis for him to be under no illusion when he raised him to power. The Cardinal would tolerate no rival in council. His great ability was equalled only by his great consciousness of it. He knew himself to have no equal, in speed of thought, in accuracy of memory, in certainty of judgment, and he probably had no equal in the Europe of his day. His despatches, lucid and intricate as coloured mosaics, his exact and delicate instructions to ambassadors and his monumental letters of advice to the King all show a mastery of detail and a sense of the political situation equally impressive for its breadth and its particularity. This political perspicacity was moreover rooted deeply in a wide general knowledge and civilised understanding of many subjects outside politics. Nothing, he held, made a man more stupid in politics than a single-minded devotion to politics alone.

Richelieu's career up to 1624 had been that of an ambitious man; he was greedy for power with a greed that could be satisfied only by the highest position in the state. He believed that he wanted that power only for the good of France or, as he would have put it, "for the glory of God and the honour of France." The next eighteen years were to show that his belief in himself was well-founded. He was a hard enemy and an exacting friend, often unscrupulous in his methods, and merciless to any who wilfully or unwittingly crossed the path that he had mapped out for France. Pomp surrounded him and the increasing glitter of unlimited wealth, as offices and benefices, amassed one upon another, accumulated in his hands. Yet even this splendour he treated only as the necessary setting for his position as the first minister of France. He was above corruption and unsparing, to his dying day, of every effort of mind and body in the service of his master. He remained always what he had always sought to be, not a rich and powerful man, but the servant of the state, or, in the words which had decked his cradle, "Armand for the King."

Chapter 4

Uncertain Tenure, 1624-1630

WHEN RICHELIEU CAME TO POWER he had to take action almost immediately in a multitude of different problems. In foreign affairs he had to consider the potential dangers presented to France by her neighbours: the powerful King of Spain and the turbulent Duke of Savoy in the south, the imperial authority on the Rhine, and the Spanish armies along the frontier of the Netherlands. He had to consider what allies were to be found among the princes of Europe; how did France stand towards the Lutheran powers of Sweden and Denmark, the Catholic power of Poland, the Calvinist power of Holland, or, for that matter, the episcopalian power of England? How did France stand and how should France stand? There was no putting off decisions; he had to take them firmly and act immediately. After fourteen years of vacillation and appeasement it was already late for the French monarchy to regain its lost credit in Europe.

But Richelieu had also to consider dangers nearer home. In one of the earliest of those lengthy bulletins of advice that he addressed to the King he wrote: "Physicians hold it for an aphorism that an internal weakness, however small in itself, is more to be feared than an external injury, be it never so large and painful. From this we learn that we must abandon what is to be done abroad until we have done what must be done at home."

The dangers at home were threefold: the irresponsible power of the nobles, the separatism of the Huguenots and the decrepit prestige of the Crown. The Cardinal planned to rebuild the French state by three measures; in his own words he set out to bring down the nobles, to break the Huguenots and to exalt the King. Of the three objectives, he put the destruction of the Huguenots first. "So long as they have foothold in France," he argued, "the King will not be master in his own house and will be unable to undertake any great enterprise abroad."

The aim was clear but there were obstacles in the way of its achievement. The statesman, unlike the historian, cannot parcel out his tasks and assign to each a convenient time and place. He is at the mercy of circumstance; he must act where, when and as he can. Thus Richelieu had to conduct an intricate policy abroad at the same time as he challenged and parried perils at home. No danger and no problem could be separately settled; he had to meet them all together.

This is the over-mastering complication of all political action. There was another complication peculiar to the ministry of Richelieu, the significance of which time has much obscured. The health of Louis XIII was always precarious, and not until fourteen years after Richelieu became his chief minister did the King become the father of a son. From 1624 to 1638—that is during the whole period of the internal conflicts in France—the heir to the Crown was the royal brother, "Monsieur" as he was officially called. This Prince, Gaston, Duke of Orléans, was the chief instigator of every revolt and the bitter enemy of Richelieu. Had the King died, Richelieu would have been the first victim of his worthless and vindictive heir. The Cardinal was perfectly aware of this. "His Majesty having no children," he wrote, "I must indeed foresee evils against which his goodness and firmness will not be able to warrant me." Furthermore the perpetual quarrels of the royal family, between Gaston and the King, between the Queen-mother and both her sons, kept the Court always in a ferment of intrigue in which it was impossible for any servant of the Crown to be always on the safest side. Richelieu, who had begun as the protégé of Marie de Medici, soon became the object of her jealousy, and in the early years at least did not always feel sure even of the King. "Now I am in your bad graces," we find him writing to Marie de Medici. "Sometimes I am on bad terms with the King and always with Monsieur and this for no better reason than that I try to serve you all with sincerity, courage and honesty."

The policy which he was conducting—the resolute, constructive and unpopular policy which was to destroy the feudal frame of society and place the Crown of France in absolute authority over the people of France—was thus worked out and carried through to its conclusions in the intermittent hubbub of the royal family's quarrels. The Cardinal's position, and more than probably his life, hung by the thread of the King's favour and the King's health. It needed cold political daring to hold so firmly to so bold a political course in so unfavourable an atmosphere.

Richelieu's first venture in foreign policy illustrated the danger of the divisions at home. He began cautiously to reorientate the French alliances, so as to draw together the potential enemies of the Habsburg power. The potential enemies were, of course, the smaller Protestant powers. Thus in 1625 European statesmen watched with a certain suspicion the reorganisation of the Protestant defences against the Habsburg crusade for a united Catholic Europe by a Cardinal of the Roman Church. Richelieu's motive was not, of course, the desire for Protestant victory but for Habsburg defeat.

A marriage alliance was negotiated between Louis' sister, Henrietta Maria, and the Prince of Wales, who was just about to succeed to the united thrones of Great Britain as King Charles I. Subsidies were offered to the Dutch in the

Netherlands and to the King of Denmark to take up the Protestant cause in Germany. The direct intervention of French troops was planned in the Val Telline. This key pass, which runs between the lands of Venice on the one side and of the Protestant province of Grisons on the other, was the most vulnerable place in the communications between the Habsburg possessions in Italy and Germany. It was, above all, the route by which Spanish and Italian reinforcements reached both the Netherlands and the German battlefronts.

The plan was at least partly successful, although the King of Denmark was defeated in North Germany and the Dutch war went sluggishly, not to say badly. French troops, in alliance with the Duke of Savoy and the republic of Venice, successfully occupied the Val Telline. The English marriage treaty was signed and the little Henrietta Maria despatched to her English husband. The Duke of Savoy, with an efficient army, overran the lands of the Republic of Genoa, the chief port and—more significant—the chief bank used by Spain in Italy.

All therefore seemed on the right road when the first internal weakness of France made itself felt. The Huguenots, consumed with their own private interests and fears, broke into revolt. They had, it must be admitted, some cause for anxiety. A Cardinal at the head of the government (even if he sought Protestant alliances abroad) did not at all reassure them. Catholic missionaries were everywhere penetrating their reserves and they were justified in believing that the renascent religious fervour of France was a force with which they could not trifle. The Cardinal was known to them as a protégé of the fanatic Father Joseph and the devout Bérulle. They may have heard of his privately expressed intention to be rid of them for he had already committed it to paper and it may have been discussed in the King's council. All the same their rebellion could not have been more inept, either for themselves as it turned out, or for the Protestant cause in Europe. For what was the immediate result? Richelieu had to withdraw

troops from the Val Telline to restore order at home.
Spanish reinforcements could once again use the passes to
feed their battlefronts in Holland and Germany. Thus no
more welcome diversion could have been made in favour
of the Habsburg crusade against heresy than had been
made by the deluded heretics of France. The delusion was
not solely theirs. In a desperate attempt to settle the French
revolt quickly and bring back Richelieu as an active
partner into the European war, the Prince of Orange, leader
of the Dutch, ordered Dutch vessels to sail to La Rochelle
to help put down the Huguenot rebellion. The Dutch seamen, stalwart Calvinists, rioted: they would not fight on
the same side as a Cardinal against their co-religionists.
Their action seemed so logical, so right, but its consequences were to be the final loss of much of Germany for
the Protestant faith.

Richelieu had to abandon his scheme of alliances and
concentrate on saving the situation in France. He played a
difficult hand with a skill which promised wonders when he
should have better cards to play. He opened negotiations
simultaneously with the Spaniards about the Val Telline and
with the Huguenots for a cessation of arms. He managed,
thanks partly to the slow distribution of news in his time, to
make the Huguenots believe that he intended to come to
terms with the Spaniards so as to have all his own forces and
Spanish help as well to overwhelm them; and he deceived
the Spaniards into thinking that he was coming to terms
with the Huguenots so as to have all their troops, as well
as his own, to bring into the Val Telline.

The results of this were the almost simultaneous treaties
of La Rochelle and of Monzon. By the first, the Huguenots
laid down their arms, by the second the Spaniards agreed
to demolish their fortresses in the Val Telline and to recognise the sovereignty of the Grisons over it. When the text
of both treaties was known, both parties were equally indignant. It did not greatly matter; Richelieu had got what he
wanted: a breathing space. He knew that he would have to
deal in the end both with Huguenots and with Spaniards.

But he hoped in future so to time his policies as not to have to deal with both at once.

This double problem had barely been carried to a temporary solution when the second of France's internal weaknesses showed itself. The nobility and the princes of the blood set about undermining the government. Richelieu's unconcealed intention to subject them to the authority of the King naturally set them on the alert against him and an edict issued in the summer of 1626 for the demolition of all fortresses not situated on the frontiers may well have been the cause of the first dangerous cabal formed against him. The edict was quite evidently aimed indifferently at Huguenot separatists, or at those great nobles who imagined they could use their cities or castles as gathering places for rebellion.

The immediate occasion of the trouble was petty enough. Gaston, Duke of Orléans did not wish to marry the noble heiress Mademoiselle de Montpensier, whom, for various dynastic reasons, it was considered suitable and safe that he should marry. His governor, who supported him in everything, was arrested and imprisoned: a harsh measure, but neither an unusual nor an unjustifiable one in the legitimate process of conducting a royal marriage to its proper conclusion. The governors of royal princes are supposed to control, not to encourage, the whims of their charges. Gaston, however, decided to be obstinate; he partly persuaded himself and partly was persuaded that he had only to intimidate Richelieu, for instance, by threatening to stab him, to get his own way. It was not altogether clear, even to him, what his own way was. But he was on very friendly terms with the Queen, and Louis himself believed that his brother wished to remain single so that, in the event of his early death, he could marry the widowed Queen. In her turn, the Queen had been suspiciously slow in repudiating the amorous advances of the English envoy, the Duke of Buckingham, in the previous year. She had allowed him to express his passion in the most unequivocal terms to her in her own bedroom. The King had, not un-

naturally, shown his displeasure, and the open estrange-
ment of the two gave rise to ugly rumours. The Queen's
beautiful and irresponsible confidante, Madame de Chev-
reuse, was certainly concerned in the plot, and she dragged
in her wake at least one besotted adorer, an empty-headed
young spark called Chalais. It is far from clear what their
ultimate intentions were; they probably did not know themselves. Chalais talked, then found he had talked to the
wrong person and, hoping to improve matters for himself
at least, decided to turn informer. There had been, he
told the authorities, some idea of intimidating, or perhaps
murdering, the Cardinal. The Duke of Orléans was involved, and others. He supplied names. The two most distinguished plotters, the King's bastard half-brothers, were
arrested. Gaston thought about making a dramatic flight,
but was too lazy. It seemed simpler to capitulate. After all,
he was only being asked to marry an heiress, not by any
means an intolerable fate. On 5th August, 1626, he was
solemnly joined in wedlock to the lady he had vehemently
rejected, by the Cardinal whom he had planned to murder:
a curious sacrament. The Queen was ordered to withdraw
from Court, and the far more guilty Madame de Chev-
reuse got off as lightly. It was rumoured, possibly with
justice, that this lovely, mischievous creature had power
over the Cardinal's heart; certainly, of all the intriguers
who plotted against him, she did it most persistently, and
always with relative impunity.

The only victim in the end was the loose-tongued
Chalais. Richelieu required his death for logical and even,
in a sense, humane reasons. He believed that if Gaston
saw a man less guilty than himself perish merely because
he had been involved in a plot on his account, he would
become ashamed of stirring up revolts to be paid for in
the blood of his friends and dependants. He reckoned without Gaston's cold-blooded egoism: he was never at any
time in his deplorable career to display the slightest com-
punction when his friends were executed while he himself,
being the King's brother, escaped unharmed.

This fantastic plot was symptomatic of the irresponsible attitude of the nobility towards the Government of their country. The remedy, as Richelieu saw it, lay in the careful reduction of their pretensions, and the systematic, and if necessary, violent contradiction of their claim to be above the law. For this reason his next move was to make the duel illegal.

The duel had for generations been the accepted way in which gentlemen settled their quarrels, but it had recently become so fashionable as to be a menace to peaceful society. High-born young men fought each other to the death for utterly frivolous reasons—for a slip of the tongue, or an imagined insult, or because they had been inadvertently jostled in a corridor. They usually took three or four seconds each, who also fought. The duel had thus become simply a kind of private warfare. It was a cause of feuds between families which broke out incessantly in bloodshed, and it made hideous the Paris streets with noisy and dangerous skirmishes. Moreover, it was an offence against the logic of civil government that murder should be punishable by death, while those privileged to carry swords might kill each other with impunity.

Richelieu advised the King to issue an edict forbidding the duel under pain of death: it was, after all, only to make the law consistent. The young nobles of France took this for a joke. Who was the King, they argued, to make it illegal for them to carry on their private quarrels in any way they chose? Montmorency-Bouteville, a notorious roaring boy, who had killed twenty-two men in duels already, demonstrated what he thought of the King, the Cardinal and the edict by fighting a duel in the Place Royale under Richelieu's own window in broad daylight. To his great surprise, he was arrested and sentenced in accordance with the new law. Immediately his family and almost the whole Court assailed the King with appeals for mercy. Louis weakened: he knew that Bouteville had been playing a schoolboy prank in defying the Cardinal. He was a silly young man, but can a man be sentenced to death for silliness? A pardon, after the fright the culprit must have had, would seem an act of reasoned mercy.

Richelieu argued with more foresight. "It may be said with truth," he wrote in a memorandum to the King, "that His Majesty and his council will have to answer for all the souls which may be lost in future by this devilish fashion if they pardon a convicted duellist." Was there, for once, a touch of personal feeling in the Cardinal's argument? His eldest brother had been killed in a duel, only a few years back. But he had a stronger argument as well. "The Cardinal realised," he writes in his memoirs, "that it was impossible to grant the young man his life without opening the door to duels and to every infraction of the law. He saw well that to pardon him would be in effect to authorise what had been forbidden by decree. It was clear that such an action would establish every kind of impunity and that, in a word, it would jeopardise the authority of the King."

"The question is," he summed it up to the wavering Louis, "do you wish to make an end of duelling or of your own power?" To pardon Bouteville would be to show that the King himself condoned the breaking of royal edicts. On 22nd June, 1627, the indignant and astonished young man mounted the scaffold. From that time onward the Cardinal had the reputation for being merciless.

While Richelieu was winning this small internal triumph, the external situation was deteriorating rapidly. The armies of the imperial Habsburg, under the all-conquering general, Wallenstein, were thrusting their way steadily towards the Baltic, while the scattered Protestant powers quarrelled among themselves. The rival Scandinavian Kings, who might together have held back this advance, would not fight side by side in the same war, and while Christian of Denmark staggered under Wallenstein's advance in Germany, Gustavus of Sweden was harvesting irrelevant laurels in Poland. Meanwhile, the English Government, failing altogether to understand the European situation, was tampering with the French Huguenots.

The marriage between King Charles and Princess Henrietta had had disappointing results. The favourite Buckingham, besotted with his own greatness and resentful of his treatment in France, had deceived himself into believing that he was the new Protestant saviour. In July 1627, an English fleet, commanded by Buckingham himself, suddenly appeared off La Rochelle and seized the island of Ré, which fronts the port. La Rochelle itself raised the standard of revolt in the confident expectation that a general Huguenot rising would follow. In the southern provinces the Huguenots, under the Duke of Rohan, rose in arms.

On the island of Ré itself, however, the fortress of Porte St. Martin held out for the King, blockaded by sea by the English fleet and besieged on land by the troops under Buckingham's command. While the King, with his army, hastened to lay siege to La Rochelle on the mainland, Richelieu was using all his endeavours to raise enough shipping in the neighbouring ports of Brouage and Sables d'Olonne to revictual the garrison at St. Martin. There was as yet no French navy at the service of the Crown but, after a summer of feverish conscription of men, of ships, of provisions, in early October the improvised French fleet successfully ran the English blockade and unloaded food and munitions into the besieged fortress. Meanwhile, the King, in the highest of spirits, for he seems always to have been happiest among his troops, was making ready for the perilous enterprise of a sally against the English on the island. The way was over the thin spit of land, uncovered at low tide, which connected Ré with the mainland. Volunteers had been selected—almost the whole army had at first volunteered—and had moved towards the water's edge when Buckingham decided not to stay the issue of combat. He withdrew with such notable military ineptitude that he lost twelve hundred men, a good half of his troops, in a rearguard skirmish with the French garrison. Buckingham himself behaved with irreproachable courage; it was the only quality necessary for a commander that the unhappy man possessed.

The position of La Rochelle, now that the English forces

had withdrawn, was desperate unless it could hold out until a new English fleet came to its help. This was impossible before the spring, and it was now November. The Huguenot revolt in the south smouldered ineffectively without diverting the royal forces from the north. Yet the Huguenot leaders in the besieged town still counted on relief from England, and believed they could endure till then. Richelieu, too, believed that help would come and that it might be formidable. The English fleet was larger than the French, which could hardly at that time be called a fleet at all, and it had still a considerable reputation left over from the time of Queen Elizabeth; besides, feeling in England was known to be running high for the relief of their Protestant brethren in France.

Since he had not enough ships to blockade La Rochelle, nor yet to challenge the English on equal terms, Louis XIII and the Cardinal conceived the astounding plan of cutting off the city from the sea by building a dyke of masonry across the mouth of the harbour. They had the labour, they had the materials and they had engineers who believed it could be done; it was certainly an astonishing feat of marine construction, which for several generations held its place among the wonders of engineering. Popular report gave the credit to the Cardinal, but it is probable that the idea originated with Louis. Both men had received some training as soldiers, and both, presumably, knew the rudiments of military engineering; both were deeply interested in the technique and minutiæ of the military profession. But Louis, more often than Richelieu, was subject to flashes of extravagant inspiration; at flickering intervals he had some of his father's genius. Whoever first thought of the plan, both were ardently engaged in its execution. It was a wet and stormy winter, but the King and the Cardinal were daily at the works, directing, watching, encouraging. Louis wished to wield a pickaxe, but the Cardinal does not seem to have approved, perhaps out of regard for the prestige of his royal office, or because he feared he might have to do the same in respectful emulation. He himself confined his efforts to advice and orders, striding up and down in cuirass, buffcoat and boots as if he had never known other accoutrements.

The huge bulwark was completed before spring came, and with spring the English fleet. Buckingham was still collecting equipment at home, but a squadron he sent out under the Earl of Denbigh warily reconnoitred the dyke, exchanged a few shots with the French ships and went home for reinforcements. This was in May 1628, and the siege of La Rochelle had already lasted over eight months. The citizens held out still in hope of English relief; it was too late to expect mercy from their King if they surrendered.

Meanwhile, in August, at Portsmouth, Buckingham was murdered. The fleet, demoralised and badly equipped, sailed under the Earl of Lindsey, a blameless and undistinguished commander. He hovered off the dyke for a few days, and then, seeing no reason to risk the lives of his unwilling men, withdrew. The Rochellois still believed the English would come back. Not until 28th October did they finally relinquish hope and capitulate, after a siege of fourteen hungry months.

The terms were annihilating: the town lost all its special privileges and its fortifications, ceased to be exclusively Huguenot, and had to give back every church to the Roman Catholic faith. All that was left to them was the bare toleration of the Huguenot form of worship. It was worth the longe siege and the gigantic labour of the dyke thus to have shattered the most valuable and the most dangerous Huguenot stronghold in France. The King made his formal entry on 1st November, and the Cardinal, august once more in priestly vestments, gave the sacrament with his own hands to the kneeling marshals of France.

But the fall of Rochelle marked only a moment of triumph in an arduous year. In Northern Italy, the Duke of Savoy, an ally as reliable as a weathercock, had found it to his advantage to veer in the Habsburg direction. Mean-

while, that pious French Duke of Nevers, whose desire to
lead a Crusade had once so endeared him to Father Joseph,
was having serious difficulty in establishing his legitimate
hereditary claim to the Italian Duchy of Mantua. The King
of Spain was most unwilling to see a French subject in
possession of this strategically important fragment of
Northern Italy: with Mantua went the fortress of Casale
in Mont Ferrat, a significant strongpoint on the route followed by Spanish troops and supplies from Naples and
Genoa to the Alps. The Habsburg Emperor, in all things
the considerate ally of the King of Spain, had therefore
denied the French Duke's right of succession and, in defiance of papal expostulations, sent an army to thrust him
out.

As soon, therefore, as La Rochelle was subdued, King
and Cardinal, with the victorious army, marched rapidly
for the Alps. Both Louis and Richelieu were in high spirits,
flushed with past triumph and confident of future victory.
The snows had not melted before, in early March 1629,
they crossed the Mont Genèvre and forced the narrow defile
of Susa into the land of the false Duke of Savoy. The Duke
had a very fine sense of drama; coming out to surrender
to the invaders, he flung himself from his horse, staggered
forward, fell on both knees in the snow, and, it was averred
by some, kissed the King of France's boots. This was felt
by almost all present to be an exaggerated courtesy.

The humiliation of Savoy thus temporarily achieved, it
remained to settle with the remnant of the Huguenot rising.
The revolt had collapsed in the south before the brutal
troops of the Prince de Condé; the restrained and princely
leader of the Huguenot party in France, the Duke of
Rohan, forced to sue for peace, can have expected only
the most drastic terms. But Richelieu deceived alike the
fears of the Huguenots and the hopes of the extreme Catholic party. He deprived the Huguenot minority of all the
civil, political and military privileges which had made them
into a separate body within the state: they were no longer
to have towns set aside for the exclusive practice of their

faith, or magistracies and law courts of their own, still less fortresses and ports. But they were still permitted the exercise of their religion. This unique mercy brought the devout party—*les dévots*—in a swarm round Richelieu's head. The Huguenots were at the King's mercy, yet they were to escape with permission to practise their religion: this was the point above all others, they argued, where the most Christian King should have taken firm and final action. How far indeed did King Louis lag behind the Emperor Ferdinand in the suppression of heresy!

Richelieu remained unmoved, and preserved the King from yielding to this influence. His strange tolerance should be ascribed to superior perspicacity rather than to inferior zeal for uniformity. He had no respect for the faith of those whom he contemptuously called *"Messieurs les prétendus réformés."* But the Duke of Rohan was a just and honourable man, a good soldier and not—like so many other French noblemen—a natural *frondeur*. Richelieu foresaw uses for him as soldier and statesman in the struggle against Spain, a struggle in which he would continue to use Protestant allies abroad. It was with a wary eye on the reactions of the Protestant powers—the Dutch, the Danes, the Swedes, the Swiss—that Richelieu spared the faith of the defeated. He saw uses, too, for a docile and grateful Huguenot minority, and docile and grateful they became under the soothing influence of Rohan, and as the result of the Cardinal's altogether unexpected mercy.

Richelieu guaranteed liberty of worship to the Huguenots. But he did not guarantee them against the infiltration of Catholic missions into their old strongholds, the founding of religious communities in their midst, the insistent, persistent pressure of a proselytising majority. He was making way for the revocation of the Edict of Nantes, and although he would probably not have approved of the timing and manner of the revocation when it came, fifty years later, he was consciously working towards the extinction of that religion, the existence of which he had temporarily maintained.

This was one of the three problems solved: the Huguenots, as a force, were destroyed. There remained other enemies, both to Richelieu himself and to the stable government of France. The Queen-mother was growing restive; she felt that her son was more and more under the direct influence of the Cardinal, and that her own power with him had waned. It was all the more exasperating, as she had originally put Richelieu forward in the belief that he would act as her own spokesman. His indifference to her wishes and whims, his increased splendour and domination since he came to power, galled her all the more, as she believed him to be only her creature. She began now to make an insistent clamour for some office of trust and value for her favourite younger son. Gaston was a good boy again: she wanted him appointed governor of Burgundy and Champagne. Richelieu would not allow it, and prevailed with the King to prevent it. Since Louis was a man of intelligence, and the provinces suggested for his fickle and treacherous brother represented the most vital part of the French frontier, the Cardinal cannot have had much difficulty in gaining his point.

Marie de Medici made her usual scene. Richelieu, either very sure of his position or feeling that his position was indeed untenable unless he could be sure of it, offered to resign. The effect was astonishing. The King showed himself his mother's equal in playing emotional parts. There were tears, recriminations, vehement, hysterical protests that he could not live without the Cardinal. It proved altogether too much for the royal confessor, who fell ill in the effort to calm the royal conscience, tossed between a mother and a prime minister. The end was a solemnly staged reconciliation between the Queen-mother and the Cardinal in the King's presence, followed by Louis' official statement that henceforward Richelieu was to have the title of "principal minister of state." It was a total victory over Marie de Medici; but Richelieu knew her too well to believe that it would be the final one.

The Duke of Savoy was, meanwhile, actively repudiating

the boot-kissing of the spring. In the winter of 1629-30
Louis marched against him for the last time. In March he
took the fortress of Pinerolo. The Duke fled; he was an old
man now and had reigned in Savoy for half a century,
earning the capriciously given soubriquet of "Great" by his
career of adventurous duplicity. But he had changed sides
for the last time. Far up in his mountains, at Rivoli, he
heard the news from his frontiers: strokes of his death-
knell tolling—Chambéry, Annecy, Saluzzo, the keys of his
country, had fallen to the French. A week after Saluzzo
fell, he died.

Just about the time of his death, Father Joseph, carrying instructions from Richelieu, arrived at Regensburg on
the upper Danube. Here the imperial Diet had been called
to set the seal on the victory of Catholicism and the Habsburg dynasty in Germany; and here Father Joseph had
come from Richelieu to make sure that the Diet broke up
without doing any such thing.

The constitution of the Holy Roman Empire was a
strange one. Although for more than a century a member
of the Habsburg family had been elected Emperor, the
German princes stoutly maintained their rights of free
election, and had to be bribed and wooed afresh at every
succession. To prevent an interregnum it was usual for
the reigning Emperor to try to secure the succession by
having the man he wanted for his heir proclaimed King of
the Romans during his own lifetime—a prince who had
once been so proclaimed by consent of the Electors of the
Diet was regarded as having the right to succeed as Emperor without further question.

The dearest wish of the Emperor Ferdinand II was to
have his eldest son thus pre-elected to the succession, and
the Diet of 1630 was called principally for this purpose.
After the spectacular triumphs of the dynasty in the field,
the election of the heir would set the official seal on the
Habsburg domination of Central Europe and re-establish
Ferdinand II in a position almost as strong as that once
held by Charles V.

It was the task of Father Joseph to dissuade the German princes from agreeing to this election. He had instructions to point out to them the dangerous power which they would thus bestow on a dynasty whose real head was the King of Spain. "His Majesty," Father Joseph was to say, "esteems that the true good of Germany lies in the country's being governed by the Germans and not by the Spaniards." This appeal to German patriotism was, naturally, not to be weakened by the least hint that, when Spanish domination was removed, French domination might replace it.

Father Joseph was strong not only in the Cardinal's but in the Pope's tacit support. The victory of the Habsburg Crusade, carrying with it the overwhelming secular power of the dynasty, could only be disastrous to the true cause of the Church: so it was argued even in Rome. He was, therefore, to prevent the German princes from agreeing to the imperial propositions for the succession, and he was also to make sure that Charles of Nevers was recognised as Duke of Mantua, with possession of Casale: two shrewd blows at the Spanish battlefront.

The operations at Regensburg were likely to be delicate. They needed prompt communications between the Cardinal and his agents; they needed also all Richelieu's attention. He could not give it to them. Circumstances at home conspired against him and, as once before, drew his attention and energies away from foreign policy. The moody King was going through one of his difficult and jealous periods, and Richelieu, as the summer advanced, felt less and less certain of his master's support. Both the Queen and the Queen-mother never ceased to ask for his dismissal; quite apart from their personal jealousy, both of them belonged to the Spanish party, and both would have preferred to see the triumph of the Habsburg.

The King had withdrawn from the Italian front gravely ill. It looked for many days as though he could not live, and when at last he began to mend, his wife and mother, who had assiduously nursed him, used his convalescence to make mischief for the Cardinal. It was not remarkable that Richelieu had thoughts only for his present peril; the King's death would have delivered him over as a powerless prey to a vindictive royal family and to King Gaston himself. It would have been the extinction of all his hopes and plans, an extinction measured against which the probable loss of his life would hardly have mattered. The King's recovery only altered and prolonged his causes for anxiety, for Louis, weak and grateful and suddenly surrounded with feminine solicitude, seemed dangerously inclined to listen to his wife and mother. Richelieu hurried to rejoin the convalescent at Lyons. Louis was nervous and cold. Richelieu sought vainly to make his peace with the Queen-mother; she refused to be pacified, would only listen to his enemies and worked daily on the King.

Tormented by such fears, Richelieu travelled back to Paris with the Court; he was in Paris when he had news from Father Joseph at Regensburg. The Mantuan affair had been too much for the French envoys. The Emperor had bluffed and hurried them into signing a treaty by which, in return for the recognition of the French Duke, the fortresses of Casale and Pinerolo were ceded to Spain. Richelieu stormed. He would repudiate the treaty, he said. Father Joseph had been cheated. As for himself, he might as well give up politics and become a monk. His agitation, recorded by the Venetian ambassador, was extreme, but it is hard to believe that it was all about a treaty that he could and would repudiate. The truth was that in the vortex of his fears lest the King should dismiss him, he had at that moment no calmer thoughts for foreign affairs.

He dared not leave the King alone with the Queen-mother. Early in November he followed Louis to her residence at the Luxembourg, and slipped into her private apartments through the unguarded door of her private chapel. "I wager," he said, smiling uneasily as he walked in on the pair of them, "that you are speaking of me." Marie de Medici, crimson with indignation, which was for once almost justified, broke into a tirade of reproaches. Richelieu, overwrought, and no longer master of himself, fell on his knees at the King's feet. Louis, finding the scene emotionally too much for his jangled nerves, ordered Richelieu to withdraw, and himself at once left the Luxembourg for the rural peace of his hunting lodge at Versailles.

The Cardinal had no doubt who had won. Neither had the Queen-mother. Richelieu believed himself lost, and Marie de Medici was so confident of it that she began at once to summon her trusted friends and to form a shadow cabinet ready for the day when Louis came out of his Versailles retreat to disgrace the Cardinal and call her back to her rightful place at his right hand, his loving and beloved mother.

It was not long before the King spoke. In his retirement at Versailles he had his young and honest chief equerry, Claude de St. Simon, and one of his able and eloquent younger ministers, Cardinal de la Valette. Both of them must have argued Richelieu's cause. Yet there is not much evidence that the cause needed arguing. Louis felt an exasperated affection and duty towards his mother, but he had no illusions about her character or her intelligence. Richelieu, with whom he had co-operated with a growing sense of confidence for six and a half years, had earned himself a place unrivalled in his esteem. As a son, he might suffer, but as a King he could not hesitate. In Louis, the King consciously, and even painfully, governed the man.

Richelieu was summoned to Versailles. For terrible moments he hesitated: there would be time to escape his doom, he could go to Havre, of which he was governor, shut himself up there . . . But he would not go to Havre; with him, too, the King's servant governed the man. Whatever the consequences, he must obey. At Versailles, he knelt speechless. Louis raised him. Both were overcome by emotion. At a signal, the witnesses all withdrew. King and Cardinal were alone together. It was their moment of emancipation, the one from the Queen-mother, the other from long uncertain tenure to the certainty of absolute dominion.

Later that evening he poured out his gratitude and relief

in an unusually impulsive note to the King. "I desire your honour," he wrote, "more than ever any servant did that of his master . . . I shall have no greater happiness in this world than in making known to Your Majesty by ever-increasing proofs that I am the most devoted subject and the most zealous servant that ever King or master had in this world. I shall live and die in this condition, being a hundred times more Your Majesty's than I am my own."

In Paris the Queen-mother's shadow cabinet evaporated; her friends fled, her palace of the Luxembourg, which for the last week had been crowded with suitors, was empty and still as the grave. But soon astonishment in political circles gave way to mockery; they had been duped, all of them, the Queen-mother and her friends in counting on victory, the Cardinal in fearing disgrace. The thirtieth of November, 1630, the day of that stormy scene between King, Cardinal and Queen-mother, became fixed in French memory as the Day of Dupes.

Chapter 5

War Underhand, 1630-1635

THE CONFIRMATION of Richelieu's power at home made it possible for him to concentrate his attention on the problems which faced him abroad. The confusion at Regensburg and the treaty signed by Father Joseph with the Emperor ceding the fortresses of Casale and Mont Ferrat troubled him relatively little. Father Joseph had succeeded in the far more important task of preventing the election of the Emperor's son as King of the Romans. He had talked the electors over to such effect that the Emperor, abandoning at last the struggle for his son's election, was forced sourly to admit that "the Capuchin has all six electoral bonnets in his hood." As for the Mantuan affair—"the treaty is null," was Richelieu's almost immediate comment and, on the argument that the ambassadors had exceeded their orders, he proceeded to treat it as such.

It is easy to lose the way in the labyrinth of European politics during the convulsions known as the Thirty Years' War. Through the criss-cross of conflicting interests and tergiversations Richelieu had, to guide him, the clue of a coherent French policy. It is important therefore to understand in simple terms what that clue was. He expressed it frankly himself more than once. "It is necessary," he wrote, "to have a perpetual design to arrest the progress of Spain, and while this nation has for its goal to augment its dominion and extend its frontiers, France should think only of fortifying herself, and of building bridgeheads into neighbouring states to guarantee them against the oppression of Spain if the occasion should arise." It would be irrelevant to attack or defend the morality of that statement, which has at least the merit of being uncoloured by hypocrisy.

As a plan of action Richelieu's statement has three parts. First, to arrest the progress of Spain; secondly, to reinforce the defences of France; thirdly, to build bridgeheads into neighbouring countries. One of these three reasons accounts for every action in the intricate foreign policy of the Cardinal. All three were the overruling considerations in the many different wars in which he seemed perpetually to be, either indirectly or directly, involved.

By Spain, he meant the Spanish-Austrian combine. The unprecedented success of the Emperor Ferdinand II in extending Habsburg power throughout Germany had, as we have seen, been of the greatest help to the King of Spain in his struggle with the Dutch because it had secured him the route down the Rhine. Richelieu's main task of arresting the progress of Spain, therefore, was to be performed in Germany. His prolonged intervention in the Thirty Years' War was directed against the Habsburg dynasty alone, and towards the control of the Rhine in particular. His second task, that of consolidating the defences of France, was to a great extent combined with his third task, that of making bridgeheads into neighbouring states. Thus, for instance, the conquest of the strongholds in Italy, and more especially in Savoy, served a double purpose, that of creating outposts on the French frontier and that of permeating northern Italy with the French King's influence to counterbalance the King of Spain's. The same was true—although the two elements were naturally not always present in equal proportions—of Richelieu's extension of French power on the German frontier, among the cities of Alsace and in the territories of the Dukes of Lorraine and Bouillon. These princes who owed allegiance to the Emperor controlled between them the whole *massif* of the Ardennes and such keys to France as Sedan, Nancy, Charleville, and Bar-le-Duc. Clearly it was essential for the safety of France that the fortresses should be in French hands and the states themselves friendly to France.

On the Spanish frontier alone was the policy purely one of defence against possible invasion. The objective here, not attained until the last year of Richelieu's ministry, was the fortress of Perpignan, a purely defensive position at the base of the Pyrenees on the French side. Within the frontiers of Spain itself infiltration was impossible, although as part of his general policy of attack on Habsburg power Richelieu kept agents both in Catalonia and in Portugal, and was successful in both districts in stimulating domestic rebellion.

The natural allies, then, whom Richelieu sought for France against Spain were the Dutch, the Protestant German princes, the Republic of Venice, the Swiss Confederation and the Kings of Sweden and Denmark. The additional allies whom he sought to win over from the Habsburg by playing on their private interests and jealousies were chiefly the Catholic King of Poland and the Catholic Duke of Bavaria. Both these princes had become more or less involved with the Habsburg crusade, but Richelieu neglected no opportunity of encouraging them to believe that their interests lay in the opposite direction, and he was intermittently successful in so doing. The Protestant power of England, which had appeared at first to be so obvious an ally against the Habsburg as to be worth securing with the prize of a French princess, turned out in the end to be valueless either as friend or foe. Jealousy of the Dutch over matters of trade and colonisation made it increasingly difficult to draw England into an alliance of which the Dutch, with their tenacious resistance to Spain, were the geographical and political keystone. The financial embarrassment of the government of King Charles I rendered him in any case useless as an active ally.

The two perpetually dangerous and doubtful quantities were the duchies of Savoy and Lorraine, both of which Richelieu ultimately succeeded in reducing to the position of satellites, though not without preliminary alarums.

The programme of attack and defence which is suggested by this summary called for three things: diplomatic organisation, military and naval forces, and unlimited resources of wealth. Richelieu was well supplied with the first. The French nation is fertile in men of quick minds and ready speech, the essential raw material for the network of negotiations, official, half-official, friendly, menacing or secret on which his policy rested. Father Joseph stood at the head of this small body of astute and loyal servants, but such men as Charnacé, who first gained the ear of the King of Sweden, Feuquières, who through long years of skilled negotiation retained this difficult northern ally, Servien and Avaux, who negotiated the final peace in Germany, all played parts of great significance in establishing the position of their country. There was one foreigner, too, Giulio Mazarini, a Sicilian, who was employed repeatedly in delicate negotiations with the Italian princes. It was he who ultimately conducted the Mantuan affair to a happy conclusion and by the secret Treaty of Turin in 1632 gained the fortress of Pinerolo for France. Brought gradually into the inner circle of the Cardinal's lieutenants, he was, under the French version of his name, as Cardinal Mazarin, to succeed to his master's place and to complete his master's work.

The second and third necessities—men and money— were less plentiful. The French army and the French navy were both still to make. As late as 1630 there was hardly a fleet worth the name, and the army consisted of a nucleus of trained regiments only. It could reduce La Rochelle; it could sustain the frontier skirmishes and siege-warfare of Italy; but it was quite unfit to take the field against the huge, disciplined forces at the disposal of the Spanish King or even of the Emperor.

The confusion and corruption in the French royal finances, although it caused continual anxiety to Richelieu, was relatively less dangerous than the lack of an army and navy. In the first place the resources of France were considerable, and with the help of fairly extensive confiscations and fines whenever a revolt, whether of nobles or of a city, provided the excuse, Richelieu managed to find the money that was needed. He also ingeniously extended and exploited the then usual policy of selling offices of state. It sometimes happened that he would create an office for some region of France, sell it advantageously and then abolish it soon after in response to the complaints of the inhabitants—against a reasonable sum of money from the complainants.

The military problem was on the way to solution before he died; the economic problem he never solved, chiefly because he never seriously attempted it. While he worked out his diplomacy with infinite forethought and built up army and navy with zealous care, he was content, in the matter of finance, to live, on the whole, recklessly from hand to mouth. In this he followed the usual practice of his generation; nor is it very easy to see how, in the midst of so many other pressing cares, he could have undertaken the difficult task of reorganising the royal budget. So long as the King had the strength to exact what was essential this fundamental disorder was not fatal to the state.

Richelieu could not wait to implement his policy until he should have built up an army equal to that of Spain. In the meantime he had to find other ways of maintaining France's position. By far the best was to continue with the policy he had begun in 1624: that of persuading other princes to put their armies at his service. French finances, with a little effort, could be stretched to subsidise these mercenaries on the grand scale.

In 1626 Richelieu had made his first essay by entering

into an alliance with the King of Denmark to oppose the imperial forces in Germany, but the King of Denmark had proved unequal to the task. By 1628 Richelieu was already making overtures of alliance to Gustavus Adolphus of Sweden.

The Swedish King was not only a soldier of unparalleled gifts, but a national leader of intelligence and popularity. He had been unwilling to enter the German war at the same moment as his rival Christian of Denmark, and this determination to choose his own time was a bad omen for the Cardinal. Gustavus Adolphus was unlikely to prove an easy ally; on the other hand, with Denmark beaten, the English useless and the Dutch unable to attend to anything but their own frontiers, he was indispensable.

The clever, ambitious King of Sweden had drawn out of his Polish war as soon as Christian of Denmark was vanquished in Germany. For the whole of the year 1629 preparations went forward in Sweden for the German war, while Richelieu's agent, Hercule de Charnacé, tried to reach an agreement with the King about the terms on which he was to be given French subsidies. There was no doubt that the King of Sweden needed the French money; the supplies, willingly voted to him by his people, for he was immensely popular, would not serve to do much more than launch and carry safely over the Baltic the huge armament that he had prepared for Germany. To prosecute the war he would need a continuous supply of French money. But if the King wanted French money the French government needed Swedish help quite as desperately and Gustavus could afford to keep the Cardinal's agent waiting for terms.

He had landed in Germany with an army of 13,000 men in June 1630. It was a small army, an admirable nucleus of well-trained men, to which he attracted numbers of Protestant German recruits as he moved across the country. Not until January 1631—two months after the Day of Dupes had confirmed the Cardinal's power in France—did he finally come to terms with the French. By a treaty

signed at Bärwalde, while he was on the march to Frank-
fort-on-the-Oder, he contracted to keep on foot an army
of 30,000 infantry and 6,000 cavalry in Germany, towards
which the French government were to pay six-monthly
subsidies. In return for thus becoming the part paymaster
of the King, Cardinal Richelieu received on paper remarkably little satisfaction. A guarantee of freedom of worship
for Catholics in Germany was secured, so that the treaty
might be represented as partly at least in the interests of
the Church. Apart from this Gustavus bound himself not
to molest any prince friendly to France—this meant the
wavering Elector of Bavaria, of whose final defection from
the Emperor Richelieu had great hopes—and not to con-
clude the war without reference to the King of France.

It was not a very satisfactory treaty and from the first
Richelieu regarded the new ally with suspicion. Christian
of Denmark had proved too feeble to beat back the Habsburg advance; Gustavus of Sweden was likely to prove too
strong to be amenable, even to his friends.

While in the spring and summer of 1631 the Swedish
King pursued his way across North Germany, sweeping
up trains of German recruits as he went and forcing the
timorous German princes to accept him as friend and protector, Richelieu was quenching the last sparks of revolt
in France.

Marie de Medici had been ordered, for the last time, to
leave the country. Gaston, her favourite son, took the occasion to withdraw to Lorraine, whence he issued inflam-
matory letters and began openly to prepare an invasion, on
the grounds that the true interests of the King, his brother,
lay in dismissing the Cardinal and recalling to his side his
mother and brother. "The prisons," declared Gaston in a
fine frenzy of indignation, "are full of the King's truest
friends. The whole country groans under the tyranny of
an arrogant churchman."

Gaston's noble sentiments were not without some popular effect. The Cardinal's policy was expensive and not
particularly comprehensible to the middle classes, let alone

the people. Furthermore, the spectacle of the King expelling his mother from Court owing to a disagreement about the chief minister distressed many honest and simple folk. Thus, when the King answered his rebellious brother by issuing a declaration on 30th March, 1631, condemning the revolt, its reasons and its leaders, the Paris *Parlement* refused to ratify it.

This was the first serious clash between Louis and the organised force of French legal opinion. Such a clash had been bound to occur sooner or later, and it was perhaps as well—for the King—that it came over the rebellion of Gaston. Whatever momentary sympathy the vapid Duke of Orléans might call forth, the lawyers of the French *Parlements* were not likely, on mature thinking, to wish to involve themselves with the fortunes of a rebel prince of the blood and rebel nobility. Their traditions and their interest alike dictated an opposite course, and the surprising thing is, not so much that they abandoned their championship of Gaston, as that they adopted it in the first place. Louis had only to behave with firmness, which was as natural to him as it was to Richelieu in the face of defiance, to reduce the Paris *Parlement* to its obedience again. He told them with considerable asperity that it was their function to administer justice and to ratify his edicts without expressing opinions on matters of which they knew nothing. Resistance to the Crown was by no means yet a tradition with these gentlemen of the gown. They had not, as their elected English counterparts had, the strong conviction that they enjoyed powerful popular support. Nor had they any means of putting pressure on the Sovereign. They were not an elected body, and, since the voting of subsidies fell not to them but to the States General, they could not enforce their opinions by withholding taxes. On this occasion the Paris *Parlement* obediently ratified the King's declaration. This was the first of the many rebuffs and setbacks by which Richelieu and his master gradually reduced these bodies to impotence.

The development of the critical faculty by the *Parlement*

was, in fact, foredoomed to sterility, for they had not the mechanism to make it fruitful, and in the then social and political state of France they could not have found—as this incident of Gaston shows—allies with common interests and sufficient political perspicacity to help them. It is a hard question to answer whether France lost more by the extinction of Parliamentary criticism than she gained by the creation of a strong and stable monarchy.

Meanwhile Gaston continued to vapour on the borders, and his mother, with the help of blandishments and bribery, escaped one dark night from her exile at Blois, crossed the frontier into the Spanish Netherlands and placed herself under the official protection of France's enemies. The situation would have been more disturbing if either Gaston or Marie de Medici had had the capacity to organise effectively. As it was, Richelieu made use of the occasion to arrest the last of the Queen-mother's supporters who was still employed by the King. This was the Maréchal de Marillac, a man of unblemished character whose only crime, as he himself pointed out, was to have been loyal to the King's mother. Richelieu, fearing an acquittal if his victim had an open trial, brought him to his country seat at Rueil and had him condemned to death on a trumped-up charge of peculation by a Court sitting under his own roof.

Meanwhile the situation in Germany was developing in the most startling fashion. For over ten years the imperial forces had been consistently victorious but on 18th September, 1631, the King of Sweden utterly shattered their armies at Breitenfeld, just outside Leipzig, and thereafter swept irresistibly across Germany. By Christmas he was on the Rhine. He was also, as far as Richelieu was concerned, completely out of control. His frankly Protestant policy—the whole war was treated by him and his publicists as a Crusade—had compromised Richelieu very seriously with the devout party among the French Catholics. He showed no signs of respecting Bavarian neutrality. He was talking openly of making himself Emperor. And he was already in so strong a position as to have no more serious need for French subsidies. In spite of repeated protests from Richelieu, in the spring of 1632 the Swedish army swept forward into Bavaria. It looked as though the power called in to settle with the Hábsburgs would become more dangerous even than they had been.

The situation was made no easier for Richelieu by the weakness of the French frontiers. Gaston had won the unstable Duke of Lorraine wholly to his side, and had, on the impulse of a genuine attraction, secretly married the Duke's sister. (His first wife had conveniently died shortly before.) Besides thus corrupting Lorraine, he had persuaded Henri de Montmorency, the Governor of Languedoc, to take arms against the Cardinal.

The news that Montmorency was in arms was acutely disquieting; he was an attractive and popular figure and his revolt coincided with rumours of rebellion among the peasantry, made restive by heavy taxation, and some unwelcome demonstrations of independence from the cities and the *Parlement* of Toulouse. But once again the wide divergence in character between the forces hostile to the increasing power of the Crown proved a fatal weakness to them. Both peasantry and cities hesitated to join the feudal banners even of the popular Montmorency; his presence in the field had the opposite effect of hastening them back to their allegiance. Montmorency, hopeless of victory, but loyal in a gentlemanly way to Gaston and to the outworn interests of his caste, advanced with his band of young noblemen, retainers and mercenaries as far as Castelnaudary, where he was utterly defeated by the royal forces. Vainly, he strove to get his death wound; instead he was taken prisoner and carefully preserved by skilful surgeons for death on the scaffold. He died with resignation and dignity, leaving to Richelieu in his will several valuable Italian pictures.

One solid advantage in foreign policy Richelieu wrung out of this conspiracy. The Duke of Lorraine was compelled to make his peace with the French King by agreeing to accept a French garrison in his capital at Nancy.

A month after the death of Montmorency, the King of Sweden was killed. Relations had been increasingly strained between him and the French for the whole of the year. He was virtually master of Germany and was planning a settlement of Central Europe with a fine disregard for French interests. He had the evident intention of making himself Emperor and of imposing a religious settlement which would restore to the Protestants all they had lost. He had carried the war ruthlessly into Bavaria in spite of his treaty of obligation to the contrary. Acrimonious disputes with the French on these and other questions were still far from settled when on 16th November, 1632, he met a soldier's death on the field of Lützen. He left in Germany a well-knit, well-officered and victorious army, and at home in Sweden a little girl of five to succeed him. The effective ruler for the child Queen Christina was the Chancellor Axel Oxenstierna, an able and a wise man, but—unlike his master—a man who could be managed.

Richelieu indeed estimated him at first too low and sent instructions to his agent, the astute Marquis de Feuquières, to build up the French position in Germany with the help of the Elector of Saxony, who he believed would, on the King of Sweden's death, be the most influential man in the Empire. Feuquières recognised immediately the Cardinal's mistake. The drink-sodden and vacillating Elector was of no more consequence after Gustavus' death than before, whereas the Swedish Chancellor carried the weight of his master's prestige and his own ability.

The Protestant princes and rulers of Germany met at Heilbronn in March 1633 to consider the situation and there formed themselves into the defensive alliance against the Emperor known as the Heilbronn League. Their deliberations were enlivened by a polite and interesting contest for power between Oxenstierna and Feuquières. Feuquières persuaded the assembled German delegates to place themselves not under the protection of Sweden but under the joint protection of France and Sweden. Next he refused to renew the Treaty of Bärwalde on the original terms. Oxenstierna could not afford to go without French subsidies, for his capacity to maintain his position in Germany rested on his ability to pay the army and thus to prosecute the war. When Feuquières insisted that in future the subsidies should be paid to the Swedish army exclusively on behalf of the Heilbronn League, Oxenstierna had to agree, although this stipulation reduced the army to the status of a mercenary force hired to do battle for the interests of others. It was a position which Gustavus had always avoided.

The plans of Richelieu, ably executed by Feuquières, the wiliest of his many lieutenants, were not complete even when he had established France as the tutelary goddess of the Heilbronn League. The imperial generalissimo Wallenstein, Bohemian by birth and a financier, rather than a soldier, of genius, was evidently discontented with the service of the Emperor. This extraordinary man, whose private wealth had enabled him to place an army at the imperial service, was inspired by immense and nebulous ambition. When he had given an interview to Father Joseph at Regensburg he had talked impressively of a Crusade against the Turks. He seems also to have dreamed of a free Bohemia under his personal authority as the middle of a Central European state stretching from the mouth of the Elbe to the Hungarian plain. His temporary dismissal in 1630 had given Gustavus Adolphus the initial advantage in his triumphant campaign, and it had been necessary to recall him in panic after the catastrophe of Breitenfeld. But the setback of his retirement had only intensified his personal ambition and weakened his loyalty to the Emperor.

A few months after the French successes at Heilbronn, Richelieu approached him. He seemed amenable to the French offers; in return for his treason to the Emperor, he was given to understand that he would be recognised as King of Bohemia. How firmly Richelieu counted on the effects of Wallenstein's treason it is difficult to say with certainty, for he must have been aware that the generalissimo was physically and to some extent mentally ill and he must have realised fairly soon that the huge army which Wallenstein believed he could bring over to the Emperor's enemies was not likely to follow him. By a counter plot the Emperor had taken care to secure the loyalty of the greater number of Wallenstein's staff. The strange drama ended with the murder of Wallenstein himself on imperial orders in February 1634.

In spite of this disappointment, the situation seemed to be working out satisfactorily for Richelieu. At home all was quiet. The Queen-mother was quiescent in exile and Gaston had been officially reconciled to the King. Montmorency was dead; the great nobles were employed in the French army or peaceably at home; the Huguenots were powerless. In Central Europe all seemed in train to resist the further aggression of the Habsburg. The Val Telline, it was true, had been open for the passage of Spanish troops ever since Richelieu had been forced to abandon it in 1628, and a large contingent under the King of Spain's brother, the Cardinal Infante Don Ferdinand, had crossed into Germany in the late summer of 1634. But it was one thing to cross *into* Germany and quite another to cross *over* Germany. Between the Spanish army and its goal in the Netherlands were massed the compact Swedish forces under Marshal Horn and the army of the allied German princes under the young and brilliant soldier Bernard of Saxe-Weimar.

Suddenly, like thunder from a clear sky, news reached the French Court, hunting at Fontainebleau in September, that the Swedish army had been broken and the German army scattered at Nördlingen near the Danube. Horn was a prisoner, Bernard with what was left of the forces had fallen back to the Rhine, and the Spanish army was marching in triumph for the Netherlands. Feelings at the French Court were divided. Richelieu himself recognised the danger and sent immediate instructions to Feuquières telling him to reassure the German princes that help would not be withdrawn in the hour of their need. But if he was anxious he was also aware of the advantages he could draw from the situation, for the heavy blow to the Swedish forces would inevitably throw the German princes more completely under his influence. But there was one acute reason for anxiety very near at hand; the Cardinal Infante was own brother to the Queen of France, Anne of Austria. As soon as he reached the Netherlands she entered into correspondence with him and was quite openly in sympathy with the Spaniards.

The Cardinal opened negotiations at once with Bernard of Saxe-Weimar and what was left of the Heilbronn League. In their extremity he offered them 12,000 troops and a substantial immediate subsidy; for return he wanted the Alsatian towns of Schlettstatt and Benfeld and the bridge-head at Strasbourg. It was a hard treaty, for Richelieu still refused to commit himself to open war, either with the Emperor or with Spain. Bernard of Saxe-Weimar agreed to it, but Oxenstierna with considerable courage refused to ratify it for the Swedish government. He calculated that the Swedes still had a position in Europe and an army of a kind left in Germany, and that Richelieu would not risk losing their friendship altogether.

The Cardinal for his part did not fully envisage the gravity of the Nördlingen disaster in its repercussions on French policy until the late autumn. There was repeated news of more troops massing in Spain and Italy and rumours of naval armaments intended for a descent on the French Mediterranean coast, still lamentably unarmed. The whole balance of power in Europe had been reversed by the joint victory of Spanish and Austrian arms at Nördlingen and the re-establishment of imperial authority on the Rhine. When, in April 1635, Oxenstierna came in person to Paris he found Richelieu more fully alive to his own danger and for that reason all the readier to moderate his terms.

Oxenstierna had only one emphatic demand. He wanted an open declaration of war from France. This, he felt, and felt rightly, would put a different face on the situation. Not

merely French money would be invested, but the honour
and prestige of the French Crown. They came to terms at
Compiègne on 30th April. The terms in France's favour
were substantially what they had been before: the left bank
of the Rhine from Breisach to Strasbourg was to be surrendered to the French Crown, but in return for this the
Cardinal promised more than the habitual subsidy. He
agreed that war should be declared on Spain.

It remained only to find a technical excuse. The Bishop
of Treves had placed himself officially under French protection three years previously; on their northward progress
into the Netherlands the Spanish forces had swept through
Treves and carried off the protesting prelate as a prisoner.
Louis XIII now formally demanded his release from the
Cardinal Infante. The request was refused. This provided
the technical excuse for a declaration of war.

International relations in the seventeenth century stood
midway between the mediæval and the modern. Most of
the devices of chivalry, the relics of personal and feudal
relations between King and King had vanished. But, with
a respect for tradition, Richelieu decided to declare war
in the correct archaic fashion. He despatched a herald and
a trumpeter to Brussels who, on 21st May, 1635, standing
in the Grande Place in the midst of an inquisitive throng,
announced, after the proper fanfare, the King of France's
just cause and threw into the crowd a formal proclamation
of war. They then set spurs to their horses and galloped
safely off.

It was the last time that this out-of-date comedy was
played in Europe. It is curious, and a little significant, that
Richelieu should have made such a point of preserving the
ancient form. The Cardinal never saw himself as an in-
novator and he liked behaviour to be on all occasions
regulated and correct. He learnt with undisguised gratifica-
tion that the French herald's performance of this elaborate
and pointless ceremony had been right in every detail.

Chapter 6

The Year of Anxiety, 1635-1636

THE CAREFUL CALCULATIONS of Richelieu were subject to the rude modification of events. He had used the Swedish army to fight the Spanish war for him in Germany until its destruction at Nördlingen. That disaster had forced on him a declaration of war before he was ready for it. The fruits of eleven years of cautious policy would be destroyed if the French army proved unequal to the strain now to be put on it. An open war with Spain and with Spain's German allies exposed not only the Pyrenean frontier but also the whole eastern frontier of France to attack, from the Channel coast, along the vulnerable flat lands of the Somme, up through the wooded Ardennes and the Vosges, as far as the Alpine borders of the Genevan Republic and the Duchy of Savoy.

It was possible that the French army would not be equal to the strain. So far, French regiments had won victories only against small forces and in limited campaigns. None knew their weaknesses better than Richelieu. Frivolity and impatience were the vices of which he fiercely accused his compatriots. "There is no people in the world," he wrote, "less suited to war than ours. Their levity and impatience in the least hardship are two failings which, unhappily, put this proposition beyond all doubt." During one of the earliest campaigns against the Spaniards in Italy, Richelieu had gloomily compared the qualities of the two nations. "If we attack feebly," he had written, "they (the Spaniards) will sustain it easily and that may force upon us a long war in which they will have the advantage, for they have the habit of endurance, just as we have the advantage in enterprises which depend for success only on the 'French fury.' " He was willing to concede that his countrymen were excellent in short, sharp, concentrated attack, but he feared that they were quite unfitted for the long war on which he had now embarked. Besides, the existing army was far too small to be able to compete in the field with the Spanish forces.

Diplomatically, Richelieu's preparations had been far more careful, and to some extent the military weaknesses of France were offset by the system of treaties which defended her borders. When Richelieu openly entered the war in May 1635 he had three important alliances: first, he had the Treaty of St. Germain of November 1634, with Bernard of Saxe-Weimar; secondly, he had a treaty of mutual support with the Dutch signed in February; thirdly, he had the treaty with the Swedes, which meant that he maintained what was left of the Swedish army in Germany, a useful diversionary force. By the summer of 1635 he had concluded at Rivoli a fourth treaty of offence and defence against the Spanish monarchy with the Italian Dukes of Savoy, Mantua, Modena and Parma.

In the first summer and autumn of the war the position on the long French frontier shifted in France's disfavour. Spanish troops moved up to occupy the Electorate of Treves, within striking distance of the passes between the Ardennes and the Vosges, themselves indifferently secured by the neutral Duchy of Lorraine. The feather-pated Cavalier at present ruling this key-province, Charles IV, was another Duke of Savoy for ambition and unscrupulousness but without the cunning and genuine ability which had distinguished the Savoyard. He had always been friendly with Gaston of Orléans—a pretty pair of rakes—and had recently connived at Gaston's marriage to his sister, a marriage repudiated by the King of France and, of course, the Cardinal. Relations were thus a little strained between Lorraine and the French court.

Richelieu despatched reinforcements immediately to Bernard of Saxe-Weimar to make sure at least of Heidelberg and the Rhenish Palatinate, if he could not be so sure of Lorraine and had already lost Treves. But even these reinforcements came too late. While the Spaniards massed to the north, the imperial forces under Count Gallas, in August, invaded Lorraine from the south. Among their polyglot ranks was the English soldier of fortune, Sydnam Poyntz, whose account is worth quoting for the impression which it gives of the brilliance and inadequacy of the French troops. "It was," he wrote, "the goodliest sight that ever I beheld, a world of brave horses and men coming up a hill in such order: and the first day they were clad all in horsemen's coats of scarlet colour and silver lace; the next day having laid by their coats they were all in bright armour and great feathers wonderful beautiful to behold." The decorative French proved, however, no better fighters and less enduring soldiers than the war-stained imperial mercenaries under Gallas. After staring at each other for three months from opposing trenches both armies withdrew. Poyntz, graphic and ungrammatical, completes his story. "The winter coming on, either side retreated, but the French rose first, by reason the French could not endure such hardness as the Germans: but all their bravery which they showed at their coming was gone, we could see at their parting neither scarlet coats nor feathers, but sneaked and stole away by little and little from their camp. And it seems most of their brave horses were eaten or dead for few we could see at their departure nor hear so much neighing of horses as when they came."

The retreat without battle was ill-advised. Gallas drew off towards Alsace, took the insufficiently garrisoned town of Zabern which guards the strategic gap in the Vosges, one of the gateways to France, and stood ready for attack in the following spring. It seemed that Richelieu's anxiety lest the French should prove unequal to the strain of long endurance was well-founded.

He guarded against the possible effect of bad news on the people by filling the *Gazette* with encouraging items. This newspaper had been started as a private enterprise by Theophraste Renaudot, a Parisian doctor, some years before. Richelieu had immediately taken the useful news-sheet under his protection and control. It served him well throughout the war. "The *Gazette* shall play its part," he noted in a letter, "or Renaudot will lose the pension he has enjoyed up to the present." There was nothing he did not know about methods of controlling editors, though his task was relatively easy as he had only one to control. The taking of the little fortress of Chatillon-sur-Saone was, for instance, celebrated as a major triumph in the obedient newspaper. It was signalised by *Te Deums* and bell-ringing to cheer the people. Richelieu himself marked the occasion by setting up two fountains with commemorative inscriptions at his country house.

The only constructive achievement of the first year of war was in the Val Telline, on which front Richelieu had astutely exploited the religious ardour of the Huguenots. A Calvinist faction in the Grisons, headed by the fanatical pastor, Jurg Jenatsch, believed that the valley might be won for the reformed religion. Richelieu despatched the Duke of Rohan, the official leader of the French Huguenots, with an army of his co-religionists, to assist the men of Grisons. The *coup* was completely successful and by the close of the year the Val Telline was occupied by French troops.

But the serious trial of strength between the French and Spanish armies was yet to come. The Flemish frontier was undermanned on the French side. Farther south, the Zabern gap, the key-pass in the Vosges, was already commanded by the enemy. At midsummer 1636 the double onslaught came. A Spanish army led by the

Cardinal Infante himself, the victor of Nördlingen, invaded from the north-east and the imperial army under Gallas poured in through the Vosges, converging fast on Paris. In response to feverish cries for help, Richelieu's German ally, Bernard of Saxe-Weimar, strove by forced marches to turn the Austrian flank as the army advanced through Lorraine. Before he could do so the Spaniards had passed Amiens, scattering the French outposts like skittles, and had occupied Corbie, the last great fortress on the road to Paris. Their outriders had galloped through panic-striken Compiègne on the night of 15th August. The suburbs of Paris were almost reached.

In the city there was panic. Refugees were already streaming west. At the council table Louis assembled his white-faced advisers. Richelieu rose first. His courage and his judgment had alike deserted him, and although he spoke with his usual incisive tone of command, the counsel which he gave was one of despair. The King and Court must at once withdraw from Paris, he said. They must place the Seine between themselves and the invaders and do what could be done to stabilise the situation after abandoning the capital. The Cardinal was suggesting that Louis should be reduced to a position of ignominious defence such as no French King had taken up towards a foreign invader since Joan of Arc pulled Charles VII out of Chinon.

When Richelieu had finished, Louis turned to his other councillors. Each in turn agreed with the Cardinal. It looked like the unanimous desertion of Paris.

It was the hour of the King. The stubborn courage of the Bourbon family may have prompted him, or a political instinct for once more certain than that of the Cardinal. Or was it the infinite strength of the anointed King, the certainty of mission and the knowledge of duty? For almost the only time in their long association Louis rejected the Cardinal's advice. It was not in his nature to make heroic gestures. He spoke without emotion, dryly, reasonably and well; the desertion of Paris, he said, would demoralise his army and his people. Briefly and with considerable military judgment he outlined the course which he wished his armies to pursue. Then, rising to his feet, turned to the youthful St. Simon, his First Equerry, and ordered him to have all ready for his departure for the front that afternoon. By nightfall he was at Senlis, midway between Paris and Corbie, a King and soldier in the front line, with his men and his people: the son of Henry of Navarre.

In Paris Richelieu had left the inauspicious council and returned to the Palais Cardinal. The King's action had startled him: it had not reassured him. He was appalled at the disaster. So great was it, so final did it seem, that his momentary despair is hardly astonishing. He had held the highest power in France for eleven anxious years; all that time, without relief, he had worked continuously towards the reduction of the Spanish monarchy and the consolidation of his master's power. He had withstood attack from within and from without, organised at home and negotiated abroad, unremittingly vigilant, alert and calculating; a myriad diplomatic threads ran back like clues from the chanceries and the battlefronts of Europe into that single, ordered brain. And now for all result a Spanish prince was a day's march from Paris with a triumphant Spanish army. The human mechanism, even an abnormal human mechanism, will stand just so much and no more. It is not surprising that the disaster which threatened, within a few days, to bring down the delicate fabric of all his plans in irreparable ruin, should have paralysed his judgment. More surprising is the fact that he was able, within twenty-four hours, to master his despair and resume the calm guidance of the state.

Father Joseph restored his vanquished spirits. The Capuchin had a stronger faith than the Cardinal. Like the King he was secure in that supranatural confidence which Richelieu, with all his gifts, had not got. The King and the monk, the one by virtue of his office and the other by nature, had that touch of the divinely unreasonable of which in Richelieu's hard, critical brain there was no trace. But whatever the panoply of Father Joseph's soul, he spoke in homely words. He told the Cardinal to show himself in the streets of Paris and, by assuming a confidence he did not feel, restore the trust of the people. "Do not behave," he urged with eloquent irreverence, "do not behave like a wet hen." *Une poule mouillée:* it was a favourite phrase of his. This salutory firmness restored Richelieu's equilibrium; while the King was rallying his forces at Senlis, the Cardinal was touring the streets of Paris to encourage the frightened citizens.

The confidence which the Cardinal did not feel was justified by events. In the south Bernard of Saxe-Weimar continued to outflank and hold the Austrian advance and in the north the Cardinal Infante fatally hesitated, giving the French time to stabilise the front at Senlis and recover their drooping spirits. With the declining year, the invaders abandoned their hopes of Paris; in early November the French recaptured Corbie and by the winter the invading armies had withdrawn.

The threat to Paris, the double invasion, the panic, the King's bold action and the withdrawal of the invaders— all had their effect on opinion in France. The anxieties of what was long remembered as "the year of Corbie" had brought home to the Parisians and to educated Frenchmen the reality of the Spanish menace, so that the Cardinal's foreign policy ceased to be something remote but became comprehensible in its broad outline to the majority of intelligent Frenchmen. It remained unfortunately incomprehensible and unpleasing to the Duke of Orléans and his faction who had used the moment of crisis to plan another attempt on Richelieu's life. He was to have been assassinated soon after he joined the King at Senlis but at the last moment Gaston lost his nerve. The conspiracy was not discovered at the time, but its existence is significant of those personal dangers from which Richelieu was never free.

Chapter 7

The Army and Navy

RICHELIEU had always feared a "war of endurance" for which he believed the French temperament unsuited. But only a war of endurance would ultimately reduce the power of Spain. His policy after Corbie seems to have been that of keeping the French army engaged in relatively small border campaigns yielding quick returns, while the serious fighting was left to the Duke of Saxe-Weimar. He had long-term plans for building up a highly-trained military caste, and planned an academy to take no less than a thousand pupils; but this came to nothing and the army in Richelieu's time was never fundamentally altered. That was to be the work of a later generation.

Nevertheless the French, however restive they became, did sustain the war of endurance surprisingly well. It was true the Cardinal made it as attractive for them as he could by the lavish ordering of military salutes, and all the processions and celebrations for which he could find excuse. The obedient Theophraste Renaudot held his *Gazette* wholly at the government's disposal and painted the glowing accounts of French successes just as the Cardinal saw fit to build them up from the despatches which reached him. Much of the *Gazette* bears the unmistakable mark of his dictated style, brief, emphatic and a little archaic.

Whatever the effect made by the *Gazette,* the eighteen months which followed "the year of Corbie" were not eventful. Bernard of Saxe-Weimar was stubbornly inactive, protesting always that he had not enough troops or enough money to cross the Rhine and carry the war into the Habsburg lands. A self-confident soldier, he was on the whole contemptuous of his French paymasters, knowing that they dared not dismiss him. He had a brisk way with armchair soldiers and civilians who presumed to advise him. On one of his visits to Paris when the Cardinal and Father Joseph were discussing the situation with him over outspread maps, the Capuchin, growing excited, began to plot out the proposed line of Bernard's march from city to city with a hurrying forefinger. "Very well indeed, Father Youssef," mouthed Bernard in his heavy German accent, "very well, if towns could be taken with finger-tips."

While Bernard advanced stubborn arguments for doing nothing, Richelieu fought the war with French troops or French diplomacy and with varying fortune on the southeastern front. The Duke of Rohan's expedition to the Val Telline had ended ingloriously. The fanatic Protestants of Grisons under the leadership of the ambitious Pastor Jurg Jenatsch had been glad of French help when it first came, but Rohan was too upright a man to be able to conceal from them that the true purpose of his government was not to protect the Protestants of the Val Telline or to extend the power of the Grisons, but simply to secure the pass against the Spaniards. Trouble broke out over the real exercise of authority in the valley; the Spaniards perceived their opportunity, opened secret negotiations with Jurg Jenatsch, and by guaranteeing the exercise of the Calvinist religion persuaded him to accept their protection rather than that of the French. Rohan had no choice but to withdraw.

A little distance away, in Savoy, Richelieu was also having difficulties. The Duchess was the sister of Louis XIII and might therefore have been expected to support her brother's policy, but when her husband died, leaving her as regent for her young son, she was at first unwilling to confirm the Treaty of Rivoli by which Savoy had been bound to France by her husband. In this question Richelieu found himself suddenly brought up against a new kind of opposition. His policy had at first had the support of the Vatican, since Pope Urban VIII, as an Italian prince, resented and feared Spanish power in Italy. But in the 'thirties Vatican policy underwent considerable modification; perpetual French intervention in northern Italy and the increasingly callous attitude of the Cardinal to the interests of the Church in Central Europe had gradually induced in Urban VIII a temper of greater suspicion towards France than towards Spain. Furthermore the "devout" party in France itself viewed the Cardinal's policy with understandable misgivings. Of his early supporters, Richelieu retained the anti-Spanish Father Joseph, but he soon lost the saintly and influential Bérulle who had once hoped so much of him. This would not have mattered so much had the King's confessor, Father Caussin, not been one of them. The whole of Richelieu's policy was suddenly seen to revolve round a delicate theological point which greatly troubled the conscience of the King.

The question was: Could absolution be granted for a sin for which the guilty party felt not contrition but attrition only? The distinction is a very definite one. "Contrition" implies the full rejection of the sin; the sin will not be continued in or committed again. "Attrition" means only the regret of the sinner arising out of fear of damnation and does not necessarily imply that the sin will be finally abandoned after absolution. This point of doctrine had been left a little vague by the Council of Trent and although the body of Catholic theological opinion was with Cardinal Richelieu in believing "attrition" or "imperfect contrition" enough, there were certain extremists, the Jansenists among them, who believed that contrition alone was valid.

The relevance of this doctrinal scruple to politics was considerable, for Louis XIII, Most Christian King of France, had signed treaties of alliance with heretic princes.

If he could not be repeatedly absolved for this continuous sin by a confessor who accepted "attrition" as sufficient ground, he would be in a very troublesome position indeed. In fact he could be restored to a state of grace only by repudiating almost the whole of his foreign policy. No wonder, therefore, that Richelieu had cause for the gravest anxiety when Father Caussin became scrupulous on the point of "contrition."

At precisely the same time the confessor of the Duchess of Savoy was urging her to resist Richelieu's pressure. It almost looked as though the tender consciences of the Bourbon family were going to undo the Cardinal's work more effectively than any Spanish victory in the field.

Father Caussin was, however, fighting a losing battle for the King's soul against the tremendous domination of the Cardinal who had, after all, a considerable body of religious opinion, including that of Father Joseph, behind him. The matter was settled by the dismissal of the over-scrupulous confessor and his replacement by one man who found it more easy to follow the Cardinal's habitual request to the King's confessors: "Do not, I ask you, meddle with matters of state."

The Savoyard business was more troublesome, but the widowed Duchess Christina found it so difficult to preserve her authority against her rebellious brothers-in-law, who all demanded their share in the Regency, that she was in the end glad to accept French help at whatever price. It proved a very stiff one; she had to yield the important fortresses of Susa, Carmagnola and Pinerolo to French garrisons and submit her policy wholly to the Cardinal's instructions. Her unhappy confessor, implacably regarded by Richelieu as the originator of the trouble, was removed from the palace to end his days in prison.

But while the advances on land were slow, Richelieu had been remarkably successful by sea. Here he had started at an even worse disadvantage, for while an army of a kind existed and the French tradition in arms was a notable one, there was, until the second quarter of the seventeenth century, no French navy and no French tradition of warfare by sea. It is necessary to go back a few years in order to trace the steps by which Richelieu effectively brought the navy into being.

As early as 1625 the Cardinal had noted, in one of his many thoughtful memoranda, that sea power in the Mediterranean would be invaluable in any war against Spain. Not only would a French Mediterranean fleet protect the coast of Provence from Spanish attack, but its presence in those waters would encourage the discontented vassal states of Spain—like Sicily and Naples—to look towards France for help should they revolt. In the following year Richelieu had to borrow ships from the English to reduce the rebellious La Rochelle, and when, in 1628, the English fleet assisted the second revolt of La Rochelle, it had only been by the extraordinary engineering feat of the dyke that the Cardinal had been able to make good the total lack of a French navy.

The lack represented a lamentable failure of the government, for naval strength was essential not only to the prosperity but to the security of the country. The coasts of France are much longer than the land frontiers, and in many places very vulnerable. Provence was raided repeatedly by the Barbary pirates, villages were sacked and men and women carried off into slavery. Nothing effective had been done for generations to prevent these periodic disasters. Neither had any government yet taken advantage of the geographical situation of France, commanding the Atlantic, the Mediterranean and the straits into the North Sea: a maritime position of considerable significance, which was to make the French in the ensuing century dangerous rivals to the English in their own element. The coasts, moreover, produced a hardy and valiant race of seamen, tenacious and stubborn in the north, wiry and resourceful in the south. The human material, the strategic bases and the geographical opportunity for the creation of a great sea power were all present.

Hitherto French mariners had been employed in the fishing trade or in merchandise. Warships were few and unorganised, not under royal command but under that of the local admirals who were responsible for the coastal defences. The governors of Brittany, of Provence and of Guienne were admirals of their own coasts, and the Lord High Admiral of France had no power save on the Channel and the North Sea. As admirals none of these high officers had been conspicuously successful.

The revolt of La Rochelle had drawn Richelieu's sharp attention to the necessity of an organised royal navy. That the only potential sea power in France should be that of the Huguenot coastal cities was clearly as absurd as it was dangerous. It was equally absurd to suppose that the then Lord High Admiral of France, that amiable Henri de Montmorency, who was to perish later on the scaffold for being concerned in one of Gaston's revolts, would have the skill or tenacity to remedy the situation.

Richelieu took the first step as early as 1626 by creating for himself the title of *Surintendant général de la navigation et commerce*. In the following year, finding that his authority was still called in question, he abolished the title of admiral, thus once again taking even a titular authority out of the hands of the nobility who had hitherto possessed it. Next he bought from their private owners the ports of Brouage, Le Havre and Honfleur, to serve as bases for the fleet that he was beginning to build. These were not the only havens to be in private hands. The reports of the commission on coasts which he next set up were illuminating. Hardly half a mile of his country's coasts belonged to the King. The valuable fishing and shipping rights of a seaboard rich in harbours and fisheries had been bartered away over the centuries. Noble landowners, the Church and the townships each had their share. Here a nobleman levied harbour dues, here a wealthy convent, here the town or village community. The piecemeal divisions of the French coast bore witness to the French Crown's long struggle for allies against its enemies. In order to maintain themselves by playing off one group of their subjects against another, French Kings had leased away the coast in bribes.

The *Ordonnance de la Marine* which abrogated all these rights was the essential first move towards the construction of a navy. It says much for the stability of the royal government that a decree so sweeping was possible without great outcry; but the submission of the privileged to their deprivation reflects also the new situation in Europe. The weakness of the French by sea was evident to any dweller on its shore; the owners of coastal privileges could not defray the costs of defending the ports and none can have known better than they how much such defence was needed, whether against piracy or against war.

The intention of the government, clearly set out in a naval programme which was promulgated as an edict in 1629, was to create an armament of at least fifty ships of war with the necessary smaller auxiliary craft. For the execution of the plan, however, Richelieu had to rely on the energy and willingness of the various coastal cities. Accordingly he sent to every port with a shipyard a command to build at least one warship for the royal service. The appeal to local pride and the competitive instinct was effective. While the great hulks were shaping under the hammers, Richelieu bought in merchant vessels and fitted them with cannon cast in Holland. The measure of buying abroad was transitional merely, for the Cardinal subscribed rigidly to the belief that there is no help like self-help. He was already establishing and extending arsenals and foundries for his navy at Brouage, La Rochelle and Brest.

The administrative organisation of the navy was not forgotten. At the head of the *Conseil de la Marine* was a controller, under him three commissaries general, under them thirty-eight ordinary commissioners, with the necessary secretaries. It was simple but sufficient. Each man knew what he had to do. Richelieu did not believe in the multiplying of small offices. The later habit of rewarding the crown's servants by creating sinecures in the bureaucracy did not come into being while he was alive.

France had the materials and the men for a powerful navy. Richelieu supplied encouragement, funds and the administration essential. Service in the King's ships was attractive to the growing population; it offered a relative security to the poor man, unknown in a time when social services were few and the docks or fishing boats offered only fluctuating or seasonal employment. Even the galleys, used for the Mediterranean fleet, drew some volunteers, although they depended chiefly on the able-bodied refuse of the gaols to man their banks of oars. (Judges were instructed to condemn to the galleys wherever possible.) A French galley-slave's life was unpleasant but he was sure of food, clothing, shelter and treatment which was at least not designed to lessen his usefulness. The degradation, crowding, filth and blasphemy of the galleys, which moved St. Vincent de Paul to found his mission to slaves, were perhaps scarcely more dreadful than the conditions to which the majority of these outcasts had been born.

By 1636 the Atlantic fleet consisted of thirty-eight ships of which twelve were over 500 tons, divided into three squadrons, those of Guienne, Brittany and Normandy. The Mediterranean fleet consisted of twelve galleys and thirteen auxiliary vessels. Both fleets were still rapidly growing; the keel of the magnificent warship La Couronne had been laid at La Roche Bernard; when she was completed she would measure 250 feet from stem to stern with a beam of thirty feet; she would carry seventy-two guns and a crew of 600 and draw 2,000 tons.

But the difficulty was not that of finding the materials or the crews. It was that of finding captains. The nobility, who were natural commanders in the army and who rapidly adapted themselves to the new honours and new disciplines of regular military employment, were useless at sea, where different qualities and a lifetime of experience were called for. The earliest officers of the French fleet were merchant captains or even pirates with a scattering of French Knights of Malta whom the Grand Master of their Order had agreed to second to the service of their native land. Admirals were in even shorter supply.

Richelieu's choice fell on the Archbishop of Bordeaux. Henri de Sourdis came of the same class of poor nobility as he did himself; he had had the same sort of training, as a man of action rather than as priest. Richelieu knew him to be a man of courage and intelligence who would carry out his orders.

There was another reason for his appointment. He had first been sent to Bordeaux as Archbishop to pit his influence against that of the Duke of Epernon, the Governor of Guienne, who particularly disliked Richelieu and his policy of centralisation. Sourdis had had an embarrassing quarrel with this obstreperous old bully almost as soon as he reached Bordeaux. The Duke had punched the Archbishop's nose and the Archbishop had excommunicated the Duke. Richelieu had intervened on the Archbishop's side and the Duke had had to apologise. The incident had not merely been a private quarrel; rather it had indicated the ill-feeling between the great nobles exercising local power almost independently of the Crown and the men of official status appointed by the government. Epernon was Governor of Guienne because of his birth and lands and family; but the Archbishop had been sent to Bordeaux to represent the central government.

A few months after the declaration of open war on Spain, Sourdis was given another and even more unclerical mission to add to his episcopal duties. He was created Admiral of the Atlantic fleet which, sailing from Bordeaux, was to reinforce the Mediterranean fleet. Spanish attack was hourly expected, for an Armada was fitting out at Barcelona and in June 1636 the Spaniards were in fact successful in seizing the Lerins Islands, whence they threatened the Provençal coast.

French operations were held up by the inevitable friction between Sourdis and the Maréchal de Vitry, who was for Provence what Epernon had been for Guienne. Disagreements about organisation and action became personal and

Vitry hit Sourdis with his cane, an outburst of temper which he was later sent to think over in the Bastille. The whole summer was thus lost and not until spring of the following year could Sourdis take effective action against the islands. But in May 1637 the French were successful in a naval action with the Spaniards and the Spanish garrisons surrendered immediately afterwards.

The battle was trivial in itself, but it was the first indication to the coast-dwellers of the northwestern Mediterranean that the French either had a fleet or knew how to use it. As such it was significant.

It was followed by a naval action of real importance in the late summer of 1638. French troops were besieging the Pyrenean fortress of Fuentarrabia by land and Sourdis was ordered to complete its isolation by patrolling the adjoining coast. In August a substantial Spanish fleet made ready to run the blockade. In the resulting engagement with the French, the Spaniards lost fourteen capital ships and three frigates by wreck or fire. It was a major disaster, which established the reputation of French naval strength. The almost total destruction of another Spanish fleet by the Dutch in the Downs in the following summer was the final blow to their sea power.

On land the French forces did less well, and Fuentarrabia, to Richelieu's disgust, resisted the besiegers until the time of year made further operations impossible. Fortunately, however, the deadlock in the Pyrenees was offset in 1638 by events on the Rhine. The dilatory Bernard of Saxe-Weimar had at length decided to move, and when he moved he did it to some purpose. He was, with all his faults as an ally, a remarkably able soldier. In early spring he suddenly drew the imperialist fire by marching up the Rhine towards the dominating fortress of Breisach; at Rheinfelden in March he overwhelmingly defeated the imperial forces, and by June had settled down to reduce Breisach by hunger. The siege lasted until the winter, to the nervous exasperation of Richelieu and the dim despair of its hungry citizens, but the end was never in doubt, for the Emperor had no sufficient army to relieve it.

All this spring and summer of 1638, however, there was another event for which the Cardinal anxiously waited. To the amazement, indeed to the frank incredulity of most of the Court, the Queen had announced herself pregnant.

The expectation of his wife's delivery as well as his own ill-health kept the King from campaigning that summer, but Richelieu was with the troops on the uneventful Flemish front at St. Quentin, when, in early September, he had news from Paris. The Queen, his informant told him, had given birth to "the loveliest prince you could wish to see." It was an extremely public birth, even for a royal prince; there was no question of a supposititious child or a simulated pregnancy. Gaston of Orléans, so long the heir presumptive, clutched at one last hope. He had the royal infant unswaddled in his presence; but there was no deception; it really was a boy. To console him, the King gave him a present of 6,000 écus. This was at Richelieu's wise suggestion, for Louis himself had no thought at the time for anything but the infant prince.

This domestic event was of the greatest political importance to Richelieu. Gaston of Orléans would now never have the opportunity of destroying his work, for if Louis died before his son grew up, a regency council could be appointed consisting of men who would be able to guarantee and continue the political achievements of his father's reign. The shadow of destruction which had overhung his policy from the time of its inception was at last lifted.

But worries from the battlefront disturbed the Cardinal in his contemplation of the happy future. The failure to take Fuentarrabia had angered him deeply; he suspected carelessness on the part of one at least of the noble generals in charge of operations. Fine as was the spirit of these aristocrats when their mettle was roused, they were still far too much inclined to bring a nonchalant indifference to the more unpleasant parts of war. Richelieu was pressing, not without cause, for the infliction of the death penalty for obvious derelictions of duty. Le Câtelet for instance had been surrendered without any resistance, because the nobleman in command had seen no good reason why he should undergo a dangerous and tedious siege. The King in council agreed that this culprit should be sacrificed but, with another touch of carelessness characteristic of this undisciplined epoch, mentioned the council decision to his equerry, St. Simon. St. Simon was a cousin of the proposed victim; his hastily despatched note of warning outdistanced the King's order of arrest by a few hours—time enough for the guilty commander to slip over the frontier and away. This kind of conduct, not intended as treachery yet fatal to the prosecution of effective war, was Richelieu's perpetual anxiety. St. Simon lost his post at Court. But he was only one among many who would have acted as he did.

Meanwhile Breisach, closely invested, held out week after week in conditions of unspeakable misery. And in Paris, to Richelieu's genuine grief, Father Joseph was taken ill. Both to Richelieu and to the Capuchin the fall of Breisach was infinitely desirable. If that fortress was once in French hands it would no longer matter about the Val Telline or the rest of the Rhine valley. The river could be effectively dominated and the Spanish lines of communication cut from Breisach alone. Therefore when it fell the Habsburg power would be crippled and Richelieu's and Father Joseph's goal of a dominant France would be within sight.

Father Joseph died with his worldly ambitions unrealised. His Cardinal's hat was on the way from Rome and Breisach was still in imperial hands when he died. But Richelieu, though he could no nothing about the Cardinal's hat, could do something about Breisach. Certain that the news would come soon, he forestalled it by twenty-four hours. Leaning over his dying friend he assured him with simulated excitement that Breisach had surrendered. Father Joseph should have been thinking of nobler things than the surrender of a German city, and perhaps he was. But whatever the effect of the news on his fading consciousness there can be no doubt of Richelieu's affectionate intention in giving it.

Breisach fell just before Christmas 1638, and Richelieu's satisfaction lasted little over a month. Early in February Bernard of Saxe-Weimar announced his intention of keeping Breisach for himself. As with Gustavus Adolphus before him, French subsidies had enabled him to secure land, in the actual possession of which he could defy the French government. He did worse; he threatened to go over to the Emperor—army, Breisach and all. Richelieu did not believe that he would really do so, not out of any loyalty to his allies and paymasters, but simply because the Emperor could not afford to pay him so well. But even if Bernard stopped short of treachery, his usefulness to the French was becoming problematical. "It is exasperating," complained Richelieu, "that His Majesty allows him 2,400,000 livres a year as well as extraordinary subsidies; yet he is not able to count on having troops proportionate to this sum according to the treaty made with the prince, nor to dispose of that army to the advantage of the common cause."

For six months, while Richelieu sent envoys to argue with him, Bernard of Saxe-Weimar remained resolute in his determination not to give up to the French Crown the city that he had won with French money and his own arms. Then, quite suddenly, in the hot summer of 1639 he died. His death was so timely that it was immediately rumoured that Richelieu had had him poisoned. There is, however, no evidence to support this belief. A certain measure of luck cannot be discounted in the history of Richelieu's career. Both with Bernard of Saxe-Weimar and Gustavus of Sweden he was fortunate. They died before they could fulfil their ambitions at the expense of his.

Bernard was the last of the great condottieri. He had held his army together, re-created and reformed it in victory and defeat, for seven years by the dominating force of his personality. He thus felt that his army belonged to him, personally, and he bequeathed it by testament like a personal possession to his second-in-command, a competent Swiss named Erlach. Erlach was more modern than Bernard. He did not propose to continue Bernard's policy of defiant independence. Instead he sold the army as a going concern to the King of France. Thus the "Bernardines," as these troops were called, were incorporated and finally submerged in the growing French forces.

With the fall of Breisach and the death of Bernard of Saxe-Weimar, the French government had become without question the dominant political force in Europe. In fifteen years, between 1624 and 1639, Richelieu had thus completely redeemed the position for France. He had conquered on land the strategic positions necessary to break down the co-ordination of the Habsburg Empire; he had created by sea a fleet strong enough to keep the Spaniards in check and he had gone far to consolidate the weak and riddled frontiers he had inherited. But the internal situation in France still gave cause for anxiety.

Chapter 8

The Internal Organization of France

WHILE THE WAR was certainly Richelieu's chief cause for anxiety he continued, as the occasion offered, to improve the internal organisation of France. It would be an exaggeration to imagine that he worked on any plan of far-reaching reform. He enunciated no theories, and although the tendency of all his actions was always in the same direciton—that of weakening local authority and strengthening the influence of the Crown—he undertook no thoroughgoing alteration of French institutions. Rather he worked by a process of neglecting or weakening some of those already in existence while strengthening others. His positive *creations* in internal administration were few. By far the most revolutionary measure had been the *Ordonnance de la Marine*. But nothing comparable to this can be found in the rest of his administration. The great institution in which he believed most passionately was the monarchy, and like many other statesmen of his epoch he conceived his duty as that of restoring a past greatness rather than of creating a new one. His ideal was the traditional kingship of a St. Louis—a ruler good and noble dispensing justice in person to all his subjects; he saw his own Louis as, above all, a father and law-giver to his people, the fountain of mercy, law, reward and punishment; a King surrounded with all the formality and dignity that the baroque age could supply and yet approachable by all his subjects. For him indeed the essential element of the King's authority was the capacity to act direct and without intervention on any subject however great or small: it must be for the King in the last resort to ratify or annul the decision of any other Court, and to load the subject at discretion with honour or with chains.

For Richelieu speed and secrecy were the essentials of political decisions. Long discussions or large bodies of councillors seemed to him merely obstructive. In his *Political Testament* he fixed the number of councillors convenient for the inner council of state at not more than four. True to his convictions, he had reorganised the Royal Council in 1630 with a very small inner group and three inferior councils for the discussion of executive details only.

The royal authority seems, so to speak, to have developed its muscles by using them: cautiously at first, but soon with more assurance. Thus the great nobles who acted as Governors of the provinces were removed and changed with increasing frequency. Thus rebels and those charged with or suspected of treason were tried before specially selected judges chosen for their known adherence to the policy of the Crown. This practice, occasional in earlier times, became the regular one under Richelieu. The most striking case was the trial of Marillac in Richelieu's own house. It was Richelieu too who first used that phrase of ill-repute *raison d'Etat,* reasons of state, to justify the infringement of any law which was temporarily inconvenient to him.

Michel de Montaigne remarked with a certain satisfaction in one of his essays that a French subject did not come into contact with the authority of the King more than once or twice in a lifetime. This freedom was the result of the loose and bewildering survival of innumerable feudal and

separatist privileges all over France. The whole tendency
of the French development had been away from a central-
ised government. Thus even such legal bodies as the *Parlement* for ratifying edicts were no less than six in number.
Moreover six of the chief provinces of France were still, at
the time of Richelieu's advent, privileged to call their own
Estates to vote exceptional subsidies, and therefore not
bound by decisions of the general elective assembly, the
Estates General. The effect of this was to remove these six
provinces—the Pays d'Etats, as they were called—which
amounted in size and wealth to one-third of France, from
the general assessment of taxes voted for the nation. Taxed
at their own rate, they paid only a tenth of the total taxes
of the country. The provinces concerned were Normandy,
Brittany, Burgundy, Dauphiné, Provence and Languedoc.

In the course of his administration Richelieu succeeded
in bringing three of these provinces into line with the rest
of France. Dijon, the chief city of Burgundy, was the scene
of serious rioting among the workers in the vineyards in
1630 when the news of the second Italian campaign was
followed by a rumour of more exceptional taxes. The
failure of the mayor to quell these demonstrations was
turned into a convenient excuse for restricting the number
of members of the town council and bringing the appointments under close royal supervision. In the following year
Burgundy made its peace with the King by selling its rights
as a Pays d'Etats. Much the same procedure was followed
in Provence, where the citizens again bought the royal
pardon for a series of riots in their principal cities by selling their political rights. Dauphiné gave the Cardinal even
less trouble, for it was simply deprived of its rights as a
Pays d'Etats by edict, Richelieu being well aware that the
hostility between the nobles and the cities of Dauphiné
was so strong that if either party protested he could call on
the other to quell them.

Two points are interesting about this policy of Richelieu's when we compare it with the coeval attempts of
Charles I to consolidate the royal authority in England.

The first is the very significant fact that each province of France (and in Dauphiné each class) was prepared to watch another robbed of its privileges with complete indifference. There was a certain *individual* resentment of the Cardinal's tyranny, as it was freely called, but there was no general opposition to it and no general conviction that the encroachments of the Crown could or should be stopped by united action. The second point is that Richelieu wisely never attempted what he knew he could not perform. He left Languedoc and Brittany strictly alone, and in Normandy, although an exceptionally bad rising of the peasants gave him an excuse to deprive Rouen of many of its privileges, the integrity of the province itself as a Pays d'Etats was not infringed. In his wisdom the Cardinal fully understood that the most damaging thing for the prestige of a despot is to attempt, to fail and to withdraw in any project whatsoever. Therefore he never struck except where he knew he would succeed; he thought it safer to have half of the land effectively under control than the whole of it subjugated in theory but not in practice.

His most famous work in internal administration was, of course, the development of the office of *intendants*. Even here he did not create the office, which already existed. The *intendant* was an officer appointed by the Crown to perform minor local functions; as Richelieu put it mildly—they were persons sent down into the country "from time to time" as emissaries from the central government. (Later of course they became resident, but not in Richelieu's time.) Gradually Richelieu placed in the hands of these emissaries the supervision of government, of legal decisions, of administration and above all of taxation which had before belonged exclusively to the noble governors of provinces, the gentry of the *Parlements* and those to whom the taxes were farmed. The *intendants* were naturally chosen for their fitness for a task which needed not only ability, but resolution, cunning and a thick skin. It is not surprising that many of Richelieu's *intendants*—hated and suspected from the first—have left legendary reputations for cruelty, injustice and rapacity. Some of them, however, were competent and conscientious: Abel Servien, for instance, who was sent to Bordeaux in 1627. He fell foul of the Bordeaux *Parlement* who showed their independence by trying to place him under arrest. Immediately the lawyers of the *Parlement* were summoned to Paris where—possibly in imitation of the noisy defiance of their King then going on in the English Parliament—they protested shrilly about their privileges. Louis XIII interrupted their president in the midst of his speech by sharply pulling his sleeve with the words, "To your knees, little man, before your master." It needed apparently only such demonstrations of authority and indifference to intimidate the *noblesse de robe*. The president knelt, the Bordeaux *Parlement* gave in and Servien remained, unmolested, to carry out Richelieu's orders in Bordeaux.

Politics and administration do not make up the whole life of a nation. What matters for its citizens are the opportunities that a society provides for the satisfaction of their aspirations towards wealth, comfort, security and the varying elements of human happiness. The administration of the Cardinal was not in the first place directed at satisfying these needs. With a frankness that is surprising even in the seventeenth century, Richelieu denied any particular intention of improving the lot of the people. "All politicians agree," he wrote in his *Political Testament,* "that when the people are too comfortable it is impossible to keep them within the bounds of their duty . . . they must be compared to mules which, being used to burdens, are spoiled more by rest than by labour."

The line of his thought was logical enough and not difficult to follow. He felt that it was the duty of citizens to work—if not as hard as he did himself, at least as hard as they could—for the prosperity of their country. His organisation of the state was therefore intended to provide conditions which would encourage thrift and enterprise in every section of the community. It was with half an eye on the revenues that they would bring in to the royal coffers that he established state-posts and stage-coaches to facilitate communications throughout France, but also with the intention of encouraging fruitful intercourse between the different cities and expediting the despatch of goods. The celebrated canal of Briare, the first big artificial water-route in France, had been begun under Henri IV and subsequently abandoned. Richelieu revived the project although, the commitments of the state being too heavy to carry this additional expense, he farmed the work out to contractors who completed it in 1638.

His economic and colonial projects were many, but his achievement here was less effective. Yet even his failures indicate his recognition of the importance of solid prosperity at home and of expansion abroad. He accepted on the whole the normal mercantile philosophy of his day, although he appears from his actions to have been influenced by the writings in political economy of that interesting French primitive in the dismal science, Montchrétien, a great advocate of colonial expansion. Richelieu believed that France would become prosperous by exporting as much and importing as little as she could, thus piling up great treasure of hard bullion. He had observed with envy, but without comprehension, the fortunes which were being made by the Dutch, a people, he noted, with far fewer exportable goods and a much smaller country than the French. France could offer the world silks and velvets which had not their equal; their manufacture in Tours, Lyons, Paris and Montpelier was watched over with paternal affection by the government. The headstrong French people, however, continued to buy cloth of all kinds in England and the Netherlands, to ornament their dress with gold and silver lace from Italy, and their houses with tapestry and paintings from Flanders, and to enjoy when they could any luxuries that took their fancy from all over the globe. Richelieu strove to stop these wanton liberties by an edict prohibiting all imports except in French vessels and all commercial transactions except between French subjects. Fortunately he had not the administrative force to make either of these prohibitions effective, since their outcome could have been only a disaster for the development of French commerce. Foreign wares continued to pour into France and the French continued to buy them direct from all manner of foreigners, but chiefly from the ubiquitous Dutch middlemen.

The same protectionist fallacy coupled with a touch of *folie de grandeur* brought Richelieu's various plans for colonisation and trading companies to nothing. The names of these ventures are so many monuments to an ambition which was not firmly enough rooted in reality. The *Compagnie du Morbihan,* founded for trade with Canada, the West Indies, Russia and the North—a far-spread charter—lasted a year. The *Compagnie de la Nacelle de St. Pierre Fleurdelysée,* which succeeded it and took almost the world for its province, died in as short a time. The *Compagnie des Cents Associés,* for Canada alone, collapsed for lack of funds. The *Compagnie des Iles d'Amerique,* although it secured for France the islands of St. Kitts and San Domingo, dragged on a bankrupt existence until it was liquidated in 1651. Numerous African companies were equally unfortunate. The East India Company staggered through its early years, but with all its achievements far in the future. The fundamental mistake in the constitution of all these companies was an excess of government interference. Apart from the companies, French trading ventures abroad were not fortunate; the Levant trade suffered badly at the hands of the Barbary pirates; and the English and the Dutch successfully contested French efforts to gain any commercial foothold in Scandinavia or the remote, mysterious Muscovy.

Yet the initial energy was not lacking. An embassy pushed as far as Moscow. French ships reached the East and the West Indies, explored the St. Lawrence, took possession of Madagascar. The early failures of the French trading and colonial ventures are a commentary on the wisdom of submitting initiative to the control of an overriding policy. Thus the trading companies were intended primarily to establish markets for French goods, not to find new goods to sell in France. They were discouraged from bringing home the produce of foreign lands and expected by the government to bring home bullion to increase the wealth of France, not luxury or exotic goods for the French people to buy. The French people, however, wanted luxuries and it was not really remarkable that, in defiance of the government, they bought eastern spices and eastern cloths and Russian furs from the Dutch and English merchants who carried them into the French ports in so much greater plenty than the vessels of the French companies were allowed to do.

Again the colonial expansion of England and the Netherlands was the mingled result of political separatism and the unregimented initiative of individuals and small groups. New England represented a withdrawal from the authority of the established Church of England but New France was only another outpost of the French church. Huguenots were not allowed to go there. The colony was conceived as a mission station which would establish the authority of the French King and the Roman Church as fully as they were established at home. This rigid attitude destroyed for France one of the great motive forces of emigration. At the time of Richelieu's death there were not more than 200 French colonists in Canada, although there was a convent, a hospital, a seminary for young Indians and a girls' school. The whole colony was nothing but an expensive mission. Its success, moreover, was still very uncertain. In 1627 the English—otherwise so markedly unsuccessful in their wars at this time—had captured Quebec without much difficulty, and had returned it only as the result of the peace treaty of 1630. Far more serious enemies than the English were the Iroquois Indians. The explorer, Samuel Champlain, when he first entered the huge territories along the St. Lawrence river, had made allies of the milder Hurons and Algonquins, friendly tribes, amenable to Christianity. France thus acquired with Canada the tribal hatreds of her people. The Dutch colonists of New Am-

sterdam, the frontiers of which touched those of New
France in the south, took advantage of the situation. They
gave firearms to the Iroquois, who, for the whole first century of Canadian history, terrorised the French colonists
and their Indian friends.

Richelieu can only in the vaguest sense be regarded as
the founder of French colonial power or commercial greatness. He had ideas undoubtedly but they were not closely
enough related to the facts of the situation. At home in
France, in Europe, where he had to meet and solve problems which were a part of his natural environment, his
sharp practical genius always controlled his vision. But in
spheres he did not understand, commerce and colonies, his
vision was altogether hazy, and amounted to no more than
a grand gesture "for the glory of God and the service of the
King." The ambitious charters of the companies he encouraged and the rigid rules within which he sought to
contain the adventurous spirits of Frenchmen indicate his
failure to resolve the problem to its practical elements.
Indeed, his understanding of political realities was not
paralleled even by an elementary grasp of economic questions. As an exporting country France had only one important market: unfortunately, this market was Spain. In
1635, with the declaration of war, trade with Spain was
naturally enough prohibited. Naturally enough . . . what
was not so natural was that Richelieu had never even considered the effect of the prohibition on French commerce.
In 1639 the prohibition had to be withdrawn.

The pell-mell confusion of the royal finances was not
made any plainer by the unregulated disorders of French
currency. Richelieu initiated a valuable reform when he
forbade local mints to issue anything except token coins
of a low denomination. At the same time a standard gold
coin was issued in Paris. The *Louis d'or* was put into circulation in April 1640. On the eve of its public appearance
the finance minister, who was aptly named Claude Bullion,
gave a dinner to celebrate the occasion. The first course
was a plateful of the new coinage. Many of the guests filled

their pockets and left immediately, lest they should be expected to disgorge their gains later in the evening.

Yet, though the *Louis d'or* remained at least as one solid
advantage to France, the commercial and economic designs
of the great Cardinal cannot be counted among his
successes.

Chapter 9

French Civilisation

LOOKING BACK over a century, Voltaire, in his history of France, recognised the time of Richelieu as the beginning of the great flowering of French civilisation. He did not attribute this effect to the Cardinal as a cause, nor indeed can it be truly said that Richelieu was the cause. The greatest statesman in the world and the most enlightened patron of the arts cannot call into being a Pierre Corneille or a Nicolas Poussin. But it is true that Richelieu gave opportunity and direction to the new tides of French genius; without him isolated triumphs would have been possible, but not the surrender of Western Europe to French taste and French genius, a surrender which was the outcome of the political domination he had created.

The influence of Richelieu was both direct and indirect. His direct influence is to be seen in the foundations which he originated or assisted, the Academy, the French Dictionary, the French Press, the *Jardin des Plantes,* the theatre and the opera, the manifold great baroque buildings whose construction he ordered, the paintings he collected or commissioned. His indirect influence was felt in the period of national self-confidence which he inaugurated, the ease and assurance with which he endowed the French and of which so much of their achievement was the fruit.

It would be an exaggeration to say that Richelieu imposed his personality upon anything so varied and vigorous as the expression of the French creative genius, then in the green springtime of its vigour. His cool reasonableness and his passion for order and symmetry were of their epoch and the movement towards regulated classicism and away from the opulent extravagances of the late Renaissance was on the way before he rose to power. But he gave to it the official approval of the Court and assured its triumph in France, just as he assured its domination throughout Christian Europe by the success of his political schemes.

It would be less than fair to Richelieu to deny that the arts held an important place in his political vision. His personal view of life was cultured, civilised and whole, and he imposed the stamp of that ideal on everything he touched. "It is not necessary," he wrote in his *Political Testament,* "that a man should attend without interruption to public affairs; on the contrary, concentration of this kind is more likely to make him useless than any other procedure." Whatever the pressure of business Richelieu maintained his balance by the judicious preservation of his leisure; he walked regularly in his garden, he listened every day to a short concert from his private musicians, and he made it a rule that the conversation before his household broke up for the night should be intelligent, unpolitical and soothing. Music, indeed, he valued above all things for its power of unravelling the knots in a tired brain. His choir and string orchestra of eight people accompanied him wherever he went, even on campaign.

It was the whim of a moment, no doubt, when he exclaimed that nothing gave him greater pleasure than the making of verses; his verses, in so far as they can be identified, are academically competent but show no great intensity of æsthetic feeling. It is still however remarkable that he should have found time to practise the art seriously at all. His collaboration with several dramatists, including

Corneille, in writing comedies has been sometimes sneered at. But it does not appear that he was particularly vain, rather that he was genuinely interested in this developing art. He should be given credit for his enthusiasm, if he cannot be allowed much for his gifts.

Richelieu was probably estimating his pleasures more accurately when he wrote in his testament that for the statesman there should be no greater pleasure than to witness the success of his plans. Certainly the tone of his letters frequently suggests a boyish excitement when his calculations are working out well; his writing, particularly to intimates, will take on an almost uncouth gaiety. His moments of transcendent happiness were moments of political triumph rather than of artistic achievement or even enjoyment. Yet he saw the arts, not as ancillary and unimportant functions of the body politic, but as essential elements in a balanced existence. Who shall say that this point of view was not a significant one in establishing what is, after all, still the dominant attitude in France?

His approach to the arts, like his approach to politics, was dictatorial. The establishment and the nature of French classical culture both derived something from the authoritarian intervention of the state; the defects of this authoritarianism can be judged better when its achievements have been considered. It was not, of course, the rigid authoritarianism perfected in our own time; it was the looser dictatorship of state encouragement and state patronage with state control as a lesser force more rarely invoked.

Moreover, the fact that the state was not an impersonal organisation but a very personal thing indeed, a King or a Cardinal, meant that the relationship between state and artist and the control exercised was still much more close to the direct relationship of patron and protégé which had dominated the arts since the Renaissance. Literature was the foremost field in which the Cardinal's influence was felt. The foundation of the Academy in 1635 served a double purpose. This remarkable institution was founded to establish a literary and linguistic orthodoxy. More than once since its foundation this august body has given support to misguided prejudices: its almost immediate condemnation of Corneille's play *Le Cid* was as bad an error as it was ever to make again. But on the whole its services to French literature have out-weighed its errors and done much to ensure for men of letters in France the official recognition and respect which, in spite of the widespread and remarkable literary genius of our nation, they have never been able to count on among the Anglo-Saxon peoples.

As to the celebrated quarrel of *Le Cid,* it has often been said that Richelieu was actuated by jealousy of Corneille's superior talent. The young dramatist had been engaged to help in a collaborative drama of which Richelieu himself wrote about 500 lines. The suggestion is that the Cardinal, indignant at Corneille's unwillingness to subdue his own talent to the level of his illustrious collaborator's, worked up the literary outcry against *Le Cid,* and set the Academy on to pronounce its formal condemnation.

The facts are different. In 1637 Corneille startled and ravished the Parisian public with a powerful and passionate drama on a Spanish theme. A young man, Rodrigue, the Cid, is required by his father to avenge an insult. The object of his father's delegated revenge is the father of Chimène, the woman whom Rodrigue loves. In the first half of the play the young man, after a bitter conflict between his love and his duty, resolves the struggle by killing his lady's father. The second half of the play transfers the interest to Chimène, who must in her turn decide between her love for the slayer and her duty to the slain. Politically speaking the play has to the modern mind obvious dangers; it was on a Spanish theme, indeed it was about the Spanish national hero, at a time when the Spaniards were at war with France. This was an aspect of it which, however, did not leap so startlingly to the eye of the public in 1637 as it would in the more nation-conscious world of today. The attack was on very different grounds.

The French theatre was in a delicate state. The *avant-*

garde of dramatists, with the full support of Richelieu, were striving to purify the old, untidy, ribald stage, to replace the sprawling dramas of intrigue and revenge, with their interludes of buffoonery and corpse-encumbered *finales,* by the restrained conventions of neo-classicism. Our English reaction to the whole matter is, of course, coloured by the fact that the old-fashioned uncontrolled drama achieved in English hands its richest and most poetic fulfilment. But the vehement reaction away from it was justified by its far more frequent and dreary excesses. The Academy was fighting for the unities of time, of place and of interest; it was fighting for a restrained and cultivated use of language, a civilised treatment of emotion and a return to classic themes. To the modern mind there does not seem much to choose between the theme of Medea murdering her children and that of the Cid fighting a duel. Infanticide, parricide and incest are frequent themes of classical legend. Yet the critics who had approved Corneille's bloodthirsty and not very poetic *Médée* turned on his first really great play.

The attack was led by two dramatists, Scudéry and Mairet, who cannot be acquitted of interested motives, or at least of jealousy. Abused by pamphlet, Corneille gave as good as he got, and called down upon himself a new attack. Scudéry appealed to the Academy, of which at the time neither he nor Corneille were members, and Richelieu asked the Academy to set up a commission to report on the play. It was the fair and reasonable thing to do. The Academy pronounced against it. Although this judgment was wrong, or at least posterity has made it seem so, it was not spiteful and it was not harshly expressed. *Le Cid* is a turbulent, passionate piece, full, as much of Corneille is full, of rough-shod writing. Its formidable sincerity and passion were not qualities which were likely to commend themselves, and certainly not to such an extent as to nullify in the minds of the critics the often impatient treatment of the forms they were striving to make respected. Great poets cannot be bound by rules; contemporary critics can be sure only of the rules and they can never be, in the nature of things, positive that they have to do with a great poet.

The only marked unfairness to Corneille came after the condemnation. Richelieu refused him permission to reply to it. Corneille was as indignant as any poet would be in the circumstances, but the necessity of putting a stop to the argument and restoring calm to the literary scene were more important to Richelieu than Corneille's feelings. Anyone who has had to do with any major literary quarrel, even in the press of our time, knows that such arguments can never be resolved: they can only be cut short. Both parties will probably feel aggrieved: one certainly will.

There is evidence that Corneille, when his temper had cooled, regarded the Cardinal more as his friend than as his enemy in the quarrel. He dedicated his next—and classically correct—play *Horace* to him, in terms of obsequious adulation. This has been sometimes represented as the action of a defeated man, a final humiliating surrender. It is not very likely. Corneille's rugged and uncompromising nature was not made to stoop. Besides, he had reason to be grateful for several material benefits procured for him by the Cardinal—a patent of nobility for his father (which meant exemption from taxes) and a small pension for himself.

The quarrel of *Le Cid* has drawn disproportionate attention to one part of Richelieu's activity. His interests embraced the whole French literary scene. It was the opening era of the *salon* and through the *salons* the ideas of the Court filtered down to wider and wider groups of the population. The *salon,* in its origin, owes nothing to Richelieu; it was the delightful creation of Catherine de Vivonne, Marquise de Rambouillet. She began her celebrated entertaining in 1613, and by the time of her death in 1643 countless other hostesses had followed her example, and the *salon* was an established feature of cultured social life. Madame de Rambouillet was interested in everything. The passport to her house was intellect only. She broke down social barriers and made the princes of the blood discourse on equal terms with bourgeois-born men of learning and letters. (The same effect was also achieved in the *salon* of the beautiful and gifted *demi-mondaine* Marion de Lorme, but here, of course, without the company of the ladies.) The special feature of Madame de Rambouillet's *salon* was the division of the company into a quantity of small rooms, opening one into the other, so that the groups could sort themselves out according to taste, and never be too large to prevent general conversation. Other conversational rules suggested themselves as time went on. It was, indeed, in these French *salons* of the seventeenth century that polite conversation truly began.

A generation later Molière was to mock at the half-educated women of the bourgeoisie who aped the literary airs of high society—Philaminte dismissing a cook who used a phrase "condemned in decisive terms by Vaugelas," and the *Précieuses Ridicules* deceived by a valet's impersonation of a member of the *beau monde*. But these pretentious ladies represented a by no means unworthy aspiration which was gradually to transform all middle-class society, on the whole for the better. Refinement and culture filtered downwards until the whole of the wealthier stratum of French society was saturated with it.

Richelieu's ambition was to make France the leader in the civilised arts of Europe. Hence the Academy; hence the stabilisation of the language in Grammar and Dictionary. The foundations were being gradually laid not only for the noble structure of the *Grand Siècle* of Louis XIV but for the long French domination of western culture.

For Richelieu the dignified setting of noble buildings and of luxurious, orderly surroundings were an essential adjunct to political greatness. He deplored—usually in vain—the sluttish conditions in which his King lived. (In this respect his advice was followed not by Louis XIII, but by his successor.) But if he could not persuade Louis to have the Louvre, his table and bed-chamber properly appointed, he could at least set an example himself of how these things should be done. The Palais Cardinal in Paris (on the site of the present Palais Royal) was beautifully constructed in a series of gracious courtyards and well-proportioned and well-distributed ante-rooms and reception rooms.

But if here in Paris the Cardinal's building served a political purpose, much that he built elsewhere seems rather to have been the fruit of that passion for building in brick or stone which so often accompanies the passion for political creation. Thus, he rebuilt the Cathedral at Luçon, and he converted the humble little village of Richelieu into a place magnificent enough to be the setting to the vast Italianate palace in which he smothered the crude, antique château where he had spent his poverty-stricken childhood. Here there were loggias, fountains, classical statues, frescoed ceilings and tapestried walls, great avenues of trees, plantations of the choicest shrubs and lawns on which peacocks sunned themselves. He took as much pains, too, for his last resting place, since he built the rich and beautiful new church for the Sorbonne, which he intended should house his tomb.

Not only in building, but in the arts of entertainment, Richelieu showed the King the way. Since nothing was done at Court to celebrate great occasions, it was at Richelieu's house that plays and masques and musical entertainments of the most varied and exquisite kind were organised to please the Court and to impress foreign ambassadors. This intensive official encouragement to music and the drama had a widespread effect in creating a new kind of audience—polite, fashionable and refined—and thereby a new kind of entertainment. The theatre became the recreation of educated men and respectable women, a place for cultivated pleasure, no longer for mere crudity and debauch.

The building fashion set by the Cardinal spread fast, and the face of Paris was rapidly transformed. It was already one of the largest towns in Europe, but had—literally—an unsavoury reputation. Sir John Suckling reported of it in 1623:

> I came to Paris on the Seine;
> 'Twas wondrous fair, but little clean;
> 'Tis Europe's greatest town.
> How strange it is, I need not tell it,
> For all the world may easily smell it,
> As they pass up and down.

It was in Richelieu's time that paving stones began to be laid in the muddy lanes, and the lanes themselves to be straightened and opened out. The bulwarks (*boulevards*) still ran along what are now the inner Boulevards. On the hill on the left bank, beyond the old square tower of St. Germain-in-the-Fields, an aristocratic suburb was already growing; the beautiful Luxembourg palace, with its formal, spacious garden, had been begun by Marie de Medici. Anne of Austria had contributed generously to the lovely convent of Val de Grace, whose stately dome and gracious outbuildings were soon to occupy the lower-lying meadows beyond the Sorbonne and the hill of St. Etienne du Mont. On the right bank of the river the boggy ground called Le Marais was rising into paved streets and handsome courtyarded houses.

On the Ile St. Louis, hitherto a bog, an intelligent speculator was beginning to build the lofty *hôtels,* some of which are standing to this day, with their well-shaped inner courtyards, broad stairways and lofty rooms. In the dark *Cité* on its central island some re-planning had begun under the inspiration of Henri IV and the old and crowded streets had given way to the simple, solid beauty of Place Dauphine. Over across the Pont Neuf, on the right bank, the shabby Louvre was gradually reconditioned. The huge reception rooms received large windows and balustrades; tapestry and gilding enriched the walls and ceilings, and great canvases by Rubens provided a majestic decoration.

The great and gracious capital, the Queen of modern Europe, as Rome had been of the old, was acquiring its shape and character. Richelieu took a native's pride in it. "The eighth wonder of the world," he proudly and flatteringly described it in a speech at the Hôtel de Ville.

Among the ancillary arts painting flourished exceedingly. Philippe de Champaigne came from Flanders to depict with his sharp, photographic eye the faces of the men who served to build the France of Richelieu. His superb portrait of the Cardinal is, fitly, his masterpiece, and we know Richelieu best in that majestic pose—the sweeping velvet robes filling the canvas, the narrow, pale face surmounting the pyramid of finery.

The greatest of contemporary French painters, Nicolas Poussin, had settled in Rome and an attempt to bring him back permanently to Paris did not succeed. Simon Vouet was the dominating painter in France and it was in his studio that Lesueur, Mignard and Charles Lebrun—who was to be the leading master of the *style Louis XIV*—learnt their craft.

A painter of a very different style was Georges de la Tour, who came from the border lands of Lorraine, and painted religious and *genre* pieces distinguished by massive and simple placing of the figures and the often dramatic use of candlelight or firelight. His models were drawn from the peasants and townsfolk of his neighbourhood. Also from Lorraine was the engraver Callot, whose marvellously incisive and expressive scenes of warfare and gypsy life are justly famous. He was patronised by Richelieu until his loyalty to his overlord the Duke of Lorraine caused him to reject commissions offered him by an enemy.

But it is to the brothers Lenain that we owe the most graphic pictures we have of the French people under Richelieu. They recorded the peasants with healthy stubborn faces and work-gnarled hands, over the evening soup bowl in their smoky homes, or sitting at noonday rest in the cornfield. They recorded also the lesser bourgeoisie, large families in good clothes with careful, keen faces.

The strongest spiritual force in France at the time of Richelieu was undoubtedly the religious revival. The Catholic revival, of which the Counter-reformation was the political outcome, was late in reaching France; it was, perhaps, all the more powerful on that account. During the whole of Richelieu's adult life, France was being swept by a great tide of religious fervour. Young men vowed themselves to charity and good works. Young girls had visions—Richelieu recounts some of them in his memoirs—and were marked with the stigmata. There was the usual mingling of hysteria, superstition and charlatanry with genuine exaltation. Richelieu himself, with his essentially practical and material outlook, leaned to the simpler and more calculating kind of devotion. His religion was too often a matter of bargaining or insurance. As a young man he implored St. John the Evangelist to cure him of a migraine in return for a mass in perpetuity. Later in his career he made himself more than a little ridiculous by having the relics of St. Fiacre brought all the way from Meaux to cure him of piles, and in May 1636, when the double attack was about to be launched on Paris, he urged the King to make special offerings to the Blessed Virgin for the French armies.

Although he respected and assisted in many of his works the one living saint whom he knew, St. Vincent de Paul, his natural predilections were for holy men of a different type. His long association with Father Joseph, for instance, was typical of his special attitude. Father Joseph was in many respects a noble and admirable character; the tragedy was that a man with so many of the strengths and qualities of a saint should have directed them to such wholly unsaintly work, and directed them in all good faith. But for Richelieu sanctity and wisdom directed to the achievement of great political designs were sanctity and wisdom *par excellence*.

It would be unfair to describe Father Joseph as a *faux dévot* in an age which produced so many truly devout men, as well as their counterfeits. Yet it is surely significant that when, a generation later, Molière drew in *Tartuffe* the classic portrait of a *faux dévot,* he included in his play a well-known story which had originally been told of Father Joseph. The scene in which *Tartuffe's* infatuated victim repeats at every account of his favourite's good health, good spirits and good fortune the phrase *"Ah, le pauvre homme!"* is a direct adaptation of a popular story of a Capuchin abbot who had asked a visitor from Paris for news about Father Joseph and, as he listened to the mounting catalogue of his worldly successes, had nodded sadly, *"Ah, le pauvre homme!"*

Again Richelieu showed extraordinary favour to the persecuted Italian Dominican Campanella, who took refuge in France, on his invitation, from the prolonged hounding of the Inquisition. This is not the place to discuss Campanella's interesting Utopian theories, his *City of the Sun.* Undoubtedly for Richelieu his merit was that he believed the King of France to be the chosen ruler who should create on earth the perfect government, civilised, priestly and authoritarian, of which he dreamed; he had also the more dubious merit of being learned in astrology. He had told Richelieu, before Anne of Austria was pregnant, that Gaston would never be King; and when the Dauphin was born he cast his splendid horoscope. It is an odd coincidence, and possibly not altogether a coincidence, that the infant who Campanella believed might realise on earth the perfect state depicted in his *City of the Sun* grew up in time to be called *le Roi Soleil.*

Richelieu's connection with the horrible case of Urbain Grandier and the possessed nuns of Loudun reflects the morbid and brutal side of the Catholic revival at its worst. Grandier, an able and domineering priest who is believed to have offended Richelieu when he was still only Bishop of Luçon, and who had certainly defended the local interests of his town of Loudun against the centralising tendencies of the government, was accused of afflicting the nuns of a neighbouring convent with demoniac possession. Possessed they certainly seem to have been, and they attributed their fits, seizures, visions and bad dreams to

Grandier because, so some of them averred, he frequently appeared to them at these times. The unhappy man, confronted by this mass of damaging evidence, persisted in vain in a plea of not guilty. He was burnt alive, after a singularly unjust and brutal trial, in August 1634. It is clear on the evidence that both Richelieu and Father Joseph were anxious for a conviction, although it is far less clear why they were thus concerned. The motive of personal vengeance is, in Richelieu's case, a little far-fetched. It is more likely that he resented Grandier's opposition to the *intendant* Labardemont (who conducted the trial) in certain matters of local importance. For Father Joseph, on the other hand, the reputation of the Capuchin order was at stake, since brothers of that order had undertaken the exorcism of the devils of Loudun. The whole story remains one of the dark places of history and of religion, an example of religious ecstasy turned to malicious hysteria and of the authority of Church and State misused to crush a single intransigent.

Yet although Richelieu's personal association with the religious revival in France was not of the highest, there were important interactions between his policy and the new spiritual vigour which flowed through the country in his time. On the one hand the stability which he was creating provided conditions in which the religious revival could flourish; on the other, the ideas and principles of the new Catholicism made way, in men's minds, for the ideas of authority and hierarchy on which Richelieu's government was based.

The impetus towards the life of religion had rarely been stronger. In Paris alone twenty new monasteries and convents sprang up in the first forty years of the century. The corrupt old orders were reformed by devout abbots and abbesses, and new ones were created—the Congregation of Our Lady of Calvary and the shining light of Port Royal. The contemplative life claimed young men and women of high rank. Richelieu's elder brother himself had felt the call. Sometimes the religious impulse took more active forms. Thus the great Père Bérulle organised the first colleges for young priests. The Oratory was founded in 1611 and the standard of church appointments began slowly to improve although Richelieu himself, on the whole, set the claims of well-born young priests higher than those of men of the people. As he pointed out, with his usual firm common sense, young men of birth knew better how to behave in society should God call them to high place in the Church. It was, however, noticeable how often he himself called churchmen to the high places of the state. He saw —again with practical common sense—that a priestly training better fitted a man to be conscientious and single-minded in the pursuit of his duty than did any other kind of education then in existence.

Just as the sanctity of St. Francis de Sales casts its brightness over the reawakening of faith in France, so the sanctity of St. Vincent de Paul casts its warmth over the reawakening of that faith to works. The wonder is how the gentle *abbé* from Provence got so many works even into his eighty-four years of life. He began in 1622 with his mission to the galley slaves at Marseilles; a little later he persuaded Richelieu to build a hospital for them. These outcasts were his first and his last care; when he had established a little succour for those of France, he built his mission centre in Paris at St. Lazare, whence ardent young priests set off for the Turkish seaports and the Barbary coasts to sustain the Christian prisoners in their chains. All his life he strove to organise charity for the poorest in society, and in some sort to lay the foundations of social services for the destitute and outcast. He founded in 1633 the Sisters of Charity, who still do the poor service and him honour. He set sisterhoods to work among friendless young girls and prostitutes, a whole mission of protection and rescue, and he created institutions for foundling children and for the aged. His influence indeed presides over the whole wide field of French charity.

Work as far-reaching but of very questionable value was done by the extraordinary Company of the Holy Sacrament. This was a secular organisation founded about 1620 by the Duke of Ventadour, a young man whose religious fervour forbade him to live with his beautiful wife except as a brother. By origin it was intended to assist the charitable mission of the Church by supplying anonymous information of worthy causes or useful works to be performed. Unhappily the anonymity of its action and the psychological results of its being a secret society, both very secret and very far spread, soon corrupted its purpose. It became in the end a harshly intolerant and persecuting force, which spied out immorality, dried up the springs of charity as far as it could towards recipients of whom it disapproved, hounded Protestants or the only casually devout, and became in the end not only a poison to human intercourse in many a small town or countryside, but the huge, organising power which at the end of the century forced the Revocation of the Edict of Nantes.

This final and retrograde expression of the French religious revival was in part also the outcome of Richelieu's unifying policy. It was a strange policy to impose on France where the vigorous expression of individuality is so marked a characteristic. Yet for that reason it very probably produced at first such fruitful results. The vehement particularities of creative French minds, thus disciplined, gave rise to a culture of enormous strength, fertility and resilience. But the pressure could not be applied for ever, and the explosion, when it came, splintered the French cultural tradition as irrevocably as it splintered the French political tradition. France, thanks to Richelieu, can never lose the elements with which he endowed the nation. But also, thanks to the aftermath of Richelieu, she will always have difficulty in becoming politically or spiritually whole.

Chapter 10

Cinq Mars, 1639-1642

THE PROCESS OF consolidation at home and abroad which took place under the administration of Richelieu is much more clear in the perspective of time than it was to those who lived through it, or even to the Cardinal himself. In the span of a lifetime, the momentary set-back may appear to be a permanent check, and the temporary disorder may seem a grave and prolonged condition. In the last chapters the solid achievements of the epoch have been grouped together and it is impossible not to deduce from them as we look back at them down the perspective of three centuries the picture of a prosperous and increasingly stable society in which the standards of polite living are at once rising and spreading and in which an enterprising and energetic bourgeoisie are creating a large measure of prosperity for all classes.

This society was no different from any other of the time in carrying with it a majority of poor and unprivileged. Through the life's work of St. Vincent de Paul, more occasionally through history and literature, we can form some idea of the conditions of the masses, but we should be mistaken if we took the worst for the average, or assumed that because things were often bad under the administra-

tion of Richelieu they were worse, or even no better, than
they had been before. The gradual establishment of internal
order in France was a valuable blessing to the peasantry,
even if it was not valued because it was not particularly
thought about. Conditions varied, just as the goodness of
the soil and the intelligence and industry of the people
varied from one part of France to another. The condition
of the people is a difficult study in this period for, so long
as they were content or at least quiescent, they were taken
for granted, and we hear of them in detail only when exceptional disasters had produced exceptional conditions.

The abominable system of farming the taxes had for its
chief result the loading of the burden on to the poorest
people, those who could not by bribery or connections persuade the assessors to lessen their contribution or leave
them out altogether. Richelieu's persistent attempts to bring
the clergy under taxation, for instance, were not successful. Thus in the end it was the peasantry in the country and
the artisans in the cities who paid for the army of Bernard
Saxe-Weimar and for Richelieu's war policy. Their accumulated *sous* were the small shot which was achieving for
France her new position in Europe. They were completely
uninterested in that position or in its repercussions on
them. They only knew that the war was interminable and
expensive. They were not literate and could not be reached
by the cheering propaganda of Renaudot's *Gazette*. It was
therefore not surprising that, in 1639, when Richelieu
toured the south-eastern frontier he found the townsfolk
and villagers loudly lamenting the war. He was deeply
perturbed. There had recently been a violent rising in
Normandy, the rebellion of the *Nu-pieds,* which had been
put down with difficulty and bloodshed. The ringleaders
had been executed. But Richelieu's comments both on
this revolt and on the discontent of the people in general
are interesting. He was not without sympathy for them in
spite of his firm belief that too much comfort would be
bad for their discipline. He had for instance abolished the
sou fees that they had to pay to register marriages, deaths

and births. But his first thought was always for the safety and prestige of the Crown. It was not so much that the state was a dominating idea with him, as that he could not conceive of any well-organised society in which authority was weak. He had been a child in the distressful chaos of the religious wars and for him always the ultimate good of society—from the peasant to the prince—lay in maintaining order by authority.

Thus Richelieu wrote to the King in the summer of 1639 reflecting on the revolt of Normandy and the discontent of the poor. "Consider the future in the light of the past and do not embark on policies of which the consequences may be so serious that you will not be able to quench the rebellion *except by shamefully revoking your own acts.*" He was, in fact, for a much more considerate and moderate management of the taxes but chiefly because, as a practical statesman, he feared that if the King did not moderate them of his own will, he would be compelled by the disorders of his subjects to do so. That, above all, was the humiliating contingency he wished to avoid.

Yet it is significant of the small influence of the great majority of the King of France's subjects that Richelieu in his huge correspondence so rarely speaks of them. It needed the revolt in Normandy and the widespread discontent of an exceptionally bad year to bring them into the forefront of his political consciousness. His more present and concrete anxieties in the internal condition of France were inspired not by the masses but by the bourgeoisie and above all by the small number of people who surrounded the King.

He had not ceased to watch the conduct of the various *Parlements,* and in February 1641 their rights and powers were rigidly set down in a royal edict. The edict asserts the guiding principles of absolute monarchy and confines *Parlements* finally to the registration of the royal will and the legal interpretation of the law. A restricted right of remonstrance still remained, but the whole tenor of the edict was to shut in finally, with rigid definitions, the actual or latent power of these bodies. The date of the edict, February 1641, has a certain piquancy, for it is contemporaneous with the opening months of the Long Parliament in England. Thus while the King of France and his first minister were successfully reducing the popular institutions of France to impotence, a few miles away across the Channel, the King of England was watching with helpless anguish while his Parliament put his first minister on trial for his life for having only attempted to do what Richelieu had successfully done.

Yet in spite of his repeated suppression of their revolts, the nobles and the enemies who still remained in the Court circle itself were the Cardinal's chief anxiety to the end.

It was true that the birth of the Dauphin in September 1638 had removed his main fear. Anne of Austria gave birth to a second son two years later. The French crown was thus secured away from the vapid Gaston of Orléans, whose succession would have been as disastrous to France as to Richelieu. It remained only for the Cardinal to ensure both himself and France against the early death of Louis by seeing that no undesirables were allowed to gather influence round the Dauphin's cot. Anne of Austria was not allowed to flatter herself that her position was any stronger at Court because she was a mother. The Dauphin's governess, Madame de Lansac, was of the Cardinal's choosing and had been imposed on an unwilling Queen. The Queen revenged herself by encouraging Gaston's bouncing ten-year-old daughter, "Mademoiselle," to think that the little prince would marry her when he grew up. Richelieu checked these pretensions at once and Mademoiselle was reduced to tears for having referred to the baby as "mon petit epoux."

Other dangers seemed quiescent. Marie de Medici, unloved and forsaken, was soon to die in exile. The King's romantic attachments had shifted during the period of Richelieu's power from Mademoiselle de Hautefort to Mademoiselle de La Fayette and back again. The gay, gambolling Hautefort was a harmless tease who liked the

King in a puzzled, innocent, downright way but was bored by his talk. Richelieu watched the melancholic La Fayette with more suspicion. She encouraged the King's chaste passion, was interested in all he said, offered advice and consolation. She was also deeply religious and belonged to those who deplored France's foreign alliance with heretics. Richelieu used his influence to persuade her that a convent for her was the only fitting end for the sad and holy passion of the King. Mademoiselle de La Fayette took the veil at the Parisian convent of the Filles-Sainte-Marie. Louis came and talked to her through the grille, but it was not quite the same thing as their sentimental consultations of old. Indeed it was on his way back from one of these interviews that a rainstorm drove him to take shelter in the Louvre with the Queen, a night's lodging of which the Dauphin was the surprising result. But Anne, even as the mother of his child, was not sympathetic to him, and shortly afterwards Mademoiselle de Hautefort resumed her interrupted ascendancy.

While these young women filled the King's erotic fancies the more stabilising element of friendship was supplied by the Duke of Saint Simon. He had first attracted Louis' attention in the hunting field when he had had the brilliant plan of bringing up the King's fresh mount head to tail with his tired horse so that Louis could change from one to the other in a single movement and without dismounting. Saint Simon has been preserved for posterity in his son's lucid prose; the direct portrait is of an old man, married late and very late a father, with the exacting eccentricities of an old bachelor, and yet an upright and noble character. Through the distance glass of the father's recollections reproduced in the son's memoirs it is possible to catch a small, clear vision of what he had been as a young man, and what his relations were with Louis XIII. Louis valued his breeding—a happy change after the assertive Luynes—his honesty and his restraint. There was also a deep and subtle private understanding between the two men; they could correspond by glances, but if they wished for a more elaborate public yet private conversation, they had their secret language, known to no one else. Rarely at a royal Court can there have been a man more disinterested than St. Simon. He respected the King's character and ability, served him with devotion and preserved his judgment from the changeable winds of fashion and favour. He had impressed the King as a boy because he continued to correspond with a friend who had been disgraced and whom it would have been politic to drop. His influence with the King was restrained, sober and incorruptible. Richelieu, whom he did not much like and never sought to propitiate, approved of him and had been known to consult him on the best ways of managing the royal moods. Loyalty to old friends, St. Simon's *forte,* can however be mistaken, and it was as the result of the warning that he gave to a friend who was about to be arrested for treason that he was dismissed from his post in the year of Corbie.

Richelieu was wise in believing that neither Mademoiselle de Hautefort at Court nor Mademoiselle de La Fayette at her nunnery could altogether fill the King's affections when St. Simon had gone. It was necessary to provide a new favourite before the King made some inconvenient selection of his own.

Richelieu's cold policy was right. It was his choice which was at fault. Some months before he had gratified Antoine d'Effiat, one of the superintendents of the treasury, by giving his elder son the captaincy of a company of guards. He now moved the boy into the King's entourage. Henri d'Effiat, Marquis de Cinq Mars, was seventeen, an ingenuous-looking, wide-eyed, well-grown youth with a boisterous vitality. Within a few months Louis' infatuation was the only news at Court. Anne of Austria, joining her husband at Fontainebleau, brought Mademoiselle de Hautefort with her in the hope of stemming this new passion. Louis was brutally frank. The lady, he said, must pretend no longer to his affections; he had given them all to Cinq Mars. His title was *Grand Ecuyer,* or Master of the Horse; he was familiarly known as Monsieur le Grand.

The great office and the King's passion went to the un-
steady head of Cinq Mars. On the threshold of manhood,
he was just discovering his power with women. That, too,
somewhat intoxicated him. It also made him contemptuous
of Louis for whom he seems to have felt little affection and
no gratitude. He knew the King's careful Puritan nature,
and loved to exasperate him by wanton extravagance of
dress, preening himself on the money he had spent or lost
at the gaming tables. He bragged of his expensive new
coach so ecstatically that the King lost his temper, called
him a spendthrift and would not gratify him by looking at
the toy. He knew the King's devout chastity, and enjoyed
boasting to him of his amorous adventures, until he had his
master writhing with disgust, fascination and jealousy. It
was said that he slipped out of the King's room even on
nights when he was in attendance and galloped from St.
Germain to Paris to sup at the lovely Marion de Lorme's,
or less reputable places. He was cruel and found early
which were the King's most sensitive places. Often things
went too far. The King and his Grand Equerry would be
heard quarrelling stridently as they paced the terraces;
Louis' only threat was one of dismissal which Cinq Mars
knew he would not carry out. In any case, he answered
back; he didn't care. He sulked; the King bored him. In
the pages of Tallemant des Réaux piteous and sordid pictures have survived: Louis in the huge tumbled bed, a
mastiff-bitch curled up at his side, kissing the favourite's
hands and crying. There would be storms and reconcilia-
tions, childishly signalised by written peace treaties given
under the hand of both parties.

Richelieu at first let things be. He even presided as
mediator in some of their more vehement quarrels. Louis
rode out to his house at Rueil, poured out his troubles to
him, shed tears even. Richelieu was soothing, talked to the
King like a friend and to Cinq Mars like a father (a habit
Cinq Mars particularly disliked) and made peace between
them. But he soon began to realise that Cinq Mars, secure
in the King's favour, already saw himself above the law.

He was planning to marry Marie de Gonzagues, daughter
of the Duke of Nevers, whose marriage to Gaston himself
Richelieu had prevented ten years before. The danger of
revolt among the resentful nobles was not yet over, nor
was the danger from the devout Catholic party, who disliked the war with Spain. It followed logically that if Cinq
Mars decided to play politics and to become the Cardinal's
rival for effective power, he would make himself the head
of the malcontents. Compared to this threat the frail persua-
sions of Mademoiselle de La Fayette or the moral influence
of Père Caussin had been nothing. Cinq Mars held the
King as no one had done before. He held the King so that
there was nothing the Cardinal could do to prevent the
sickeningly familiar formation—nothing except keep himself informed.

They clustered about the new favourite, wasps about to
swarm: the old gang again, swaggering Gaston, the stupid
Duke of Bouillon, the ambitious young fry of the nobility.
There was covert and open insolence to the Cardinal,
secret meetings, whispering groups in corridors. Cinq
Mars mimicked Richelieu's infirmities to the King and, it
was said, the King laughed. On whatever feeble grounds,
the arrogant young man became convinced that he had
only to get rid of the Cardinal to be able to rule the King
and France himself. The plot arranged between him and
his friends was much the same as usual, only bolder and
more treacherous for there was now open war with Spain
so that to coquette with the Spanish court was incontro-
vertibly treason.

The state of Spain was now nearly desperate. On the
Netherlands frontier the French were already in Arras,
and the Cardinal's agents, offering and giving French subsidies, had stirred up the Duke of Bragança's successful
revolt in Portugal so that this whole great section of the
Iberian peninsula had separated once again from Spain.
On the other side of the kingdom, the Catalans were in
full revolt and had proclaimed Louis XIII Count of Barcelona and their protector. In the circumstances a counter-

intervention to stir up troubles in France seemed the only fitting answer.

Gaston was to raise the revolt in Sedan, the key fortress just beyond the French frontier which belonged to the Duke of Bouillon; the Duke of Bouillon was to place the entire French army in Italy (of which he was in command) at the disposal of the rebels. The Huguenots of the Cevennes were to revolt and the Spaniards, by a secret treaty signed with Cinq Mars, were to furnish the rebels with 12,000 infantry and 6,000 cavalry, together with the munitions and money necessary for the revolt. In return they were to have the fortress of Sedan, thus gaining an entry into France itself which would compensate twice over for the loss of Breisach. It was the stupid overturning of all those years of diplomacy and war through which Richelieu had sought to consolidate the frontiers of France.

Richelieu was informed of every movement in these complex and long-drawn negotiations with the enemy. His secret service never failed him in matters of this kind. But he dared not strike until he had such proofs as would convince the King beyond all question. He feared to the last moment the ascendancy of the favourite, and an abortive arrest on insufficient evidence would have weakened his own position, perhaps irreparably.

The rebellion was ripening during the campaign of 1642. The main of the French army was operating on the Pyrenean front; since in the south the gaps in the defences had been stopped at Casale, Susa and Pinerolo, there remained only, on the Spanish frontier itself, the dangerous fortress of Perpignan. If this could be taken, every southern gap in the French defences would be sealed.

A macabre royal procession followed the armies that spring to the scene of battle, for Louis, always the soldier son of his soldier father, was set on going and Richelieu dared not let him and the favourite out of his sight. The King and the Cardinal were both dying men. Richelieu travelled in a litter, his body devoured by rodent ulcers, one of which paralysed his right arm; parchment-faced, wasted to a skeleton, he seemed already to be living by will-power alone. The King, his master, was ill and better from day to day; he was never well and had not been well for years. But there were days and even weeks together when he could stand, ride, walk, go through, with bloodless complexion and weary gesture, the pantomine of normal life. His doctors wound up and kept in order, by daily ministrations, the bodily machine which had long ceased to operate of its own accord.

As these two decrepit wrecks made their ceremonious way to join the armies, the agents of the favourite tried and failed to kill the Cardinal: once at Lyons and once at Narbonne. His loyal and careful guards forestalled the blows. But at last his health finally gave out, and with it, almost, his courage. He had to stay behind while the King and his favourite went on alone. He kept two confidential secretaries, Noyers and Chavigny, to carry his letters and instructions to his master and, alternately, to keep watch on the situation in the King's surroundings. He pursued these watchdogs with weary, anxious, harried letters. As soon as one sore on his arm closed, another opened. His surgeons wanted to operate, but "I have neither strength nor courage to let them," the exhausted patient wrote to Noyers. His servant answered with reassuring news of the King's behaviour and comfort for the sick man. "Whither are we all going," the good man consoled him, "if not home to Him of whom Saint Augustine writes: *'Tu solus requies.'* "

By the time this letter reached the Cardinal his spirits had rallied. He was not thinking any more of his last rest, but intensely of the political matter in hand. He was now merely fractious about his crippling illness. "My surgeons say I am getting better but I do not notice it," he complained. He was, however, collecting steadily on his sick bed the reports and documents he needed from his spies to confront the King with the proof of the favourite's guilt.

On 10th June the tone of his letters to Noyers changes to an almost light-hearted raillery. The faithful secretary had not reported from the King's household for a day or two. Richelieu reproached him for neglecting to keep informed "a person who, like myself, has a passion for affairs of state." This sudden cheerfulness marked the arrival at Arles of Chavigny, Richelieu's other confidential secretary, with documents incriminating Cinq Mars: nothing less than a copy of the secret treaty just concluded between the conspirators and the Spaniards. It took Richelieu about twenty-four hours to arrange the documents so as to tell their story clearly, and to add his own comments. Then he despatched Chavigny to join the King at Narbonne. To the end he still both feared and pitied the King's infatuation. "I implore the King," he wrote, "not to be distressed but to put his trust in God." Chavigny reached Narbonne very early on 12th June; the King was yet abed but gave him audience as soon as he was up. By ten in the morning all was finished; he could write to the Cardinal "all measures have been taken according to your advice."

Some accounts relate that Louis had received the messenger with the favourite at his side. "Monsieur le Grand," said Chavigny, "I have something to say to the King alone." Whatever the truth of this, Cinq Mars realised while Chavigny was with the King that he was discovered. He did not risk blustering matters out with the King; tacitly admitting his guilt, he had vanished from the royal household before the King's order for his arrest was given. Late that night a house-to-house search in Narbonne revealed his hiding-place. He was hurried away under guard to the castle of Montpelier.

The loose coalition of ambitious, stupid men fell to pieces with the favourite's arrest. The Duke of Bouillon and the principal confidant of Cinq Mars, Monsieur de Thou, were seized the next week. Gaston was politely detained. As the King, deep in melancholy, returned to Paris, Richelieu, still bedridden, collected the necessary information for the trial of the conspirators. Twice Cinq Mars tried to escape from Montpelier before he was moved under close guard to Lyons for his trial with the other prisoners. They were questioned and for a little while maintained a gentlemanly silence about each other's guilt. Then Gaston—as always—spoke. After he had lucidly accused everyone concerned with him in the plot, there was no need for heroics on their part. Richelieu arranged embarrassing confrontations, ordering every detail of the lengthy examinations from his distant sick-bed. The Duke of Bouillon, who hoped to save his life, grovelled. Cinq Mars blustered; after four years of passionate friendship, he knew the King's vindictive temper so little that he seems to have counted on a pardon.

All this while the French troops were still before Perpignan, and when Richelieu at last began the weary journey northward from Provence, couriers from this unsatisfactory battlefront followed his course all the way with the latest news. He progressed with lugubrious pomp, towed up the Rhone in a barge "on which had been erected a wooden cabin hung with branched crimson velvet on a background of gold. In the same barge there was also an ante-room hung in the same fashion; before and behind were ranged a great number of his guards in scarlet cloaks. His Eminence lay in a bed hung with purple taffeta. Before him went a little boat to mark the fairway, and immediately behind it a boatload of arquebusiers and their officers. At every island they came to, the soldiers landed to see if there was any suspect on it and, finding none, they would mount guard on its banks until the Cardinal's barge had passed by. Behind the Cardinal's barge a little covered boat was attached in which was Monsieur de Thou, the King's prisoner . . . On the banks of the Rhone marched two companies of light cavalry . . . there was a fine foot regiment too which came into the cities where His Eminence was to spend the night. When his barge touched the shore, first they set up a wooden bridge from the bank to the barge. After they had tested it to see if it was safe, they took up the bed on which His Eminence lay . . . Six strong men carried it on two poles . . . to the house where he was to lodge. But the strangest thing of all was

that he entered the houses by the windows, for, before
he came, his masons knocked down the window frames
and made openings in the walls of the rooms where he was
to lodge, and built up a wooden ramp from the street to
the opening in the wall of his room. In this way, in his
travelling bed, he was carried through the streets and up
the ramp to the room which had been prepared for him,
hung by his servants with crimson and purple damask
and rich furnishings . . . His room was guarded on all sides,
in the cellars and at the doors and even in the attics."

The huge purple bed with its cadaverous burden was
carried into Lyons on 5th September. Five days later Cinq
Mars finally broke down and admitted everything. He had
recognised at last that against the evidence of the Duke of
Orléans and the Duke of Bouillon his denials were in vain.
But he remained impenitent. He could not see that he had
committed treason. For him, a stubborn, ignorant boy,
hatred of the Cardinal was enough to justify communicat-
ing with the Spaniards and bartering his country's frontier
to the enemy in time of war. His reason was at least ex-
cusable in this: he had only the same attitude to political
right or wrong as many another conservative nobleman;
he believed it was his privilege to pursue the policy he
thought best whatever his King might command. But he
had no defence beyond this; what he had done he had
done out of pure vanity and pure hate. Nothing in his
conduct or his confession suggests that any desire for a
nobler liberty or championship of the oppressed of any
class or nation had crossed his mind. These were later
ideas attributed to him by romantic writers of the nineteenth century. He was no martyr in freedom's cause, he
had no ideal to oppose to the Cardinal's enlightened tyranny; nothing but a stupid resentment.

The less attractive elements of his character were visible
almost to the last. He spent much of his time, in the intervals of his trial, negotiating for the sale of the reversion of
his office as Master of the Horse. He incriminated his only
real friend, the luckless François de Thou, who had been

towed to Lyons in the little boat behind the Cardinal's
barge and whose only crime was that he had concealed the
plot, of which he had been made the unwilling confidant.
When Cinq Mars heard, at seven o'clock in the morning of
12th September, 1642, that he and François de Thou were
sentenced to death and were to die that day on the same
scaffold he broke into pettish anger. He was Marquis de
Cinq Mars, he protested, and would not die on the same
scaffold with a commoner. In the five hours which separated his sentence from his execution, he recovered his
sense of proportion. By midday he was at peace with his
faithful friend, with the world and with his Creator. He
contrived to ring down on his four years of power and
twenty years of life a curtain which would have done
honour to a better play.

On the same day the couriers from the Spanish front
brought the long-delayed, long-expected news. The French
army had entered Perpignan. The double risk was over:
the conspirators were dead and the Spaniards defeated.
Richelieu did not allow his pleasure in this crowning triumph to disturb the orderly course of his thoughts. Apart
from more serious affairs of state, he was busied about the
sale of the late Queen-mother's effects at the Luxembourg
Palace. The King had refused to buy them in, which Richelieu regretted, partly because it did not look well that the
King should let his mother's possessions be dispersed, and
partly because he felt the shabby Louvre could do with
some extra plate and hangings. On the day of Cinq Mars'
execution he was writing to Noyers with directions to buy
the best things at the Luxembourg at least temporarily for
the Palais Cardinal. Only when he had succinctly given
these instructions did he give the day's great news. "Perpignan is in the King's hands; and Monsieur le Grand in
the other world . . . These are two effects of God's goodness towards the King and the state."

Within a few hours, Richelieu had seen the triumph of
both his policies. There would be factions among the
nobility yet, and there was eighteen years of the Spanish

War still to come. But all was set in motion, surely and certainly, for the emergence of France as a united, modern state, and for its establishment as the greatest power in Europe. As the majestic travelling bed jolted forward on its progress towards Paris in that autumn of 1642, bearing the great Cardinal home to die in the city where he had been born, he must have felt as sure as mortal man can feel that he had achieved his life's work.

Chapter 11

The Testament of Richelieu

THE CARDINAL in his prodigious litter reached Paris by early November. He was taken to his great house near the Louvre, the Palais Cardinal, where for a few more weeks his painful existence dragged on. He can hardly have expected to recover, but he continued his lucid direction of the state to the end. There were loose ends of the Cinq Mars business to be tidied away. The Duke of Bouillon could buy his pardon by the cession of his town of Sedan, another valuable frontier post. The friends of Cinq Mars must be exiled from the Court so that no festering places for new revolt should be left. The wretched King, a prey to disillusion and despair, must be perpetually strengthened in the conviction of the favourite's unworthiness, lest remorse—of which he now showed signs—lead to mistaken leniency to his friends. Richelieu fed him with further evidence of Cinq Mars' widespread treason and continual ingratitude. The military appointments must be made for the spring campaign of the following year; Richelieu advised that a young prince of the blood, Condé's eldest son, the Duke of Enghien, be given command on the Flemish frontier. He was still in favour of trusting the Duke of

Bouillon's gifted younger brother, Turenne, with an important subsidiary command.

Not until the first week of December did the progress of his disease at last make all work impossible. For hours at a time he sank mercifully into coma, and was so weak when he was conscious that he could no longer keep his mind fixed on public affairs. Recognising the conclusion of his political life, he sent his resignation to the King. Louis refused to accept it: his greatest servant was to die, as he had lived, first minister of France. He came himself to tell him so, sat for a long while at his bedside with his hand in the Cardinal's, and fed to him at intervals small spoonfuls of egg-yolk. Homely and formal, melancholy and absurd, this farewell after eighteen years of joint government, of risks surmounted, decisions taken, dangers faced in each other's company, bears witness in its every recorded detail to the human affection of the King for his minister. These were the last moments of a long friendship.

After the King had left, Richelieu asked his niece, the Duchess of Aiguillon, to withdraw; her tears perhaps disturbed the serenity with which he wished to meet his end, but he put it more courteously: he preferred that she should not distress herself by seeing his sufferings. At the last he turned away from the outward signs and privileges of his greatness. The parish priest attended his last hours. *Etant né Parisien comme je suis* . . . he had sometimes liked to boast. Now he was dying not only in the city, but in the very parish where he had been born; the magnificent palace, enriched with treasures from all the civilised world, was built over the ground on which his parents' modest dwelling had once stood. The *curé* of St. Eustache had baptised him, and the *curé* of St. Eustache gave him extreme unction. His thoughts, after the King left, turned only to the hereafter; it was as though that astonishing concentration of mind which had been his especial gift in politics now enabled him to expel politics utterly.

A story told soon after the Cardinal's death records that, when he was asked to pardon his enemies, he replied: "I

have none except those of the state." But no ear-witness
heard him say these words. They sound so typical (indeed
they occur in one of his letters), yet they are false to the
last pre-occupations of that lofty mind. He had said, long
before, when arguing against the troublesome conscience
of the King: "Man is immortal; his salvation is hereafter;
the state has no immortality, its salvation is now or never."
He had seen to the salvation of the French state and it
troubled him now no more. His mind was fixed on his immortal soul.

With audible intensity he declared his convinced Christian belief, and wished that he had had a thousand lives to
give them all for the faith and the Church. It was a little
after this last asseveration that he fell into unconscious-
ness, lying very still, with now and again a hard, sighing
breath. In the darkened room, among the flickering candles,
his servants passed to and fro round the bed where his
confessor watched him. Towards midday on 4th December,
1642, he gave a deep, shuddering sigh, and while his confessor intoned *In manus tuas domine . .* , yet another. Then
the silence fell again. They held a candle close to the dis-
tended nostrils; the flame never moved. The lucid mind
was for ever dark.

The great Cardinal lay in state for nine days, the waxen
face and waxen hands, alone of the withered human body,
to be seen among the voluminous purple and crimson of
towering bed and flowing robes. His cardinal's hat and
ducal coronet were placed at his feet, and between them,
symbol of that faith in which he had so strangely and so
sincerely lived and died, a monstrance with a silver cross.
On either side of him a choir of monks chanted the peni-
tential psalms, and at his head the Captain of his Guard,
in black, stood sentinel.

On a dark winter evening he was carried across the
Seine to his last resting place. Over the Pont Neuf marched
the solemn cortège, the torchlight flickering above them in
the wintry air and below in the wintry river; so with all
the ceremonial furniture of death he was carried past the

place where a quarter of a century before he had applauded the desecration of his protector Concini's corpse.

He was buried in his own great Church of the Sorbonne, and there, under the huge monument of bronze, his bones lie still.

The great Cardinal's death filled Western Europe with rumour and speculation. Even in England, absorbed by its own Civil War, half a dozen lampoons appeared within a few months of his death. "The torment and the ornament of his age," wrote an English pamphleteer, "France he subdued, Italy he terrified, Germany he shook, Spain he afflicted, Portugal he crowned, Lorraine he took, Catalonia he received, Swethland he fostered, Flanders he mangled, England he troubled, Europe he beguiled. Then shalt thou admire that he is shut up now dead in so small a space, whom, living, the whole earth could not contain."

Richelieu left two valuable records behind him. The first was his *Political Testament,* a compact memorandum on the French state with maxims for its guidance. The second was his *Memoirs.* Both were widely read, and the maxims and sentiments found in them were long current in the vocabulary of politics. An English edition of the testament appeared under the title of *The Compleat Statesman* in 1695 and was several times reprinted. Richelieu had intended the original as a manual of instruction for Louis XIII after his death and much of it relates to the special problems of the French monarchy in his time, and more especially to the peculiar character of the King. It seems to have been written at different times and only assembled into its final form after his death by someone who did not remove the inconsistencies caused by the various dates at which the different sections were composed. It resembles an enlarged version of one of those weighty memoranda which the Cardinal regularly addressed to his master and which are to be studied in Avenel's handsome edition of his *Letters.* Yet there are also rules for policy and reflections on statesmanship that have a more general bearing. They lack the stylised finish of the maxims for which the *salons* of France became famous but they have the flavour of authentic wisdom. Thus, urging on the King the necessity of making gracious speeches, he writes: "Wounds inflicted by the sword are more easily healed than those inflicted by the tongue." His maxims of state are typical and usually terse:

Secrecy is the first essential in affairs of state.

To make a law and not to see it put in execution is to authorise what you have yourself forbidden.

In popular opinion, matters falsely presented in fine words are very willingly accepted as true.

A good minister, he argued, needed the four qualities of capability, fidelity, courage and application, but he added, "great men are more often dangerous than useful in the handling of affairs . . . Presumption is one of the greatest vices a man can be guilty of in public employments, and if humility is not required in those who are designed for the conduct of states, yet *modesty* is absolutely necessary; since it is most certain that those who have the greatest gifts are sometimes the least capable of taking advice."

"In judging crimes against the state," he wrote, "it is essential to banish pity." But his maxims—even this last— were not meant to be of perpetual validity and general application; he absolves the reader from regarding them as anything but direct advice tendered at a certain time to a certain King, for, he writes, "the capacity of counsellors does not require a pedantic knowledge: none can be more dangerous in a state than those who will govern kingdoms by the maxims they find in books."

The *Memoirs,* which first appeared eighteen years later under the title *Histoire de la Mère et du Fils,* are not exclusively his work and their authenticity has been disputed. There seems, however, to be very little doubt that he had intended to write *Memoirs* to vindicate his conduct, and that he had placed the necessary private and official papers at the disposal of the Bishop of St. Malo, who had worked on them for several years in Richelieu's household, and often with Richelieu's supervision. It was he who in the end completed and published the work. The *Memoirs* are thus in substance the story of Richelieu's rise to power and ministry up to 1630, recorded as he would have wished it recorded and bearing in its arrangement, and from time to time in its style, the character of his genius.

A legacy of more immediate significance to France was Cardinal Mazarin. He had first come across this astute Italian as far back as 1628, had enticed him from the papal service and, after long experience of his discretion, had had him appointed to the Royal Council a few months before he died. Mazarin succeeded him as the King's first minister and, on the death of Louis XIII five months later, as first minister to the regency.

Mazarin had Richelieu's civilised lucidity. He had not Richelieu's powerful analytical mind. He could not have begun Richelieu's far-spread foreign policy; he could and did guide it to its conclusion. In May 1643 the young commander Enghien, Richelieu's last appointment, broke the Spanish army at the battle of Rocroi. It never recovered either its efficiency or its prestige. A year later the Emperor and the King of Spain agreed to open negotiations for peace in Germany and the Netherlands. They lasted four years. In October 1648 the peace of Westphalia was concluded to the satisfaction of France. Alsace was ceded to the French Crown. The western frontier was consolidated from Strasbourg to the Flemish border. It would remain for the child King, Louis XIV, when a man, to carry that consolidation farther south, through Franche-Comté to the lake of Geneva. The ascendancy of France was already achieved.

Not until 1660 did a crippled Spain at last give in; Richelieu had rightly said that endurance was a Spanish virtue. But the Peace of the Pyrenees formally confirmed the triumph of France. The young Louis XIV met his bride, the Spanish Infanta Maria, on the frontier of the two kingdoms, just as his father, forty-five years earlier, had met

his bride, the Spanish Infanta Anna. The earlier marriage
sealed the subservience of France to Spain; the later marriage sealed the defeat of Spain by France. Whatever saving clauses the marriage treaty contained, everyone knew
that the young Louis was gaining with his bride claims to
the Spanish Netherlands and to the Spanish Crown itself
which he would not hesitate to assert when the time should
come. Sure enough the next decades saw the French frontier claw eastwards into what had been the Spanish Netherlands, enveloping Arras, Lille and Dunkirk; and the
second decade of the eighteenth century saw a Bourbon
king on the Spanish throne itself. The developments set
in motion by Richelieu had run their course.

Richelieu's monument is written in the history of France
from 1642 to the present time. His work has proved so
vital that it is hard to estimate it fairly because the account
is not yet closed.

He had found the French a vigorous but divided people;
he had found France inadequately armed, poorly policed,
inefficiently governed, yet with potentialities of order, good
government and military greatness; he had found the
French genius a fruitful, uncultivated soil. He left the
French a conscious nation; he left France efficiently governed and equipped for peace and war; he left the native
genius a marvel of horticulture, soon to be the model of
Europe. All the elements of which the powerful French
civilisation was made were present in jarring confusion in
1624. Without Richelieu they would never have been sifted
and sorted and brought into effect. The poet Chapelain, in
a courtly ode composed in 1633, apostrophises the Cardinal with the words *Ton nom seul aux Français redonna
l'asseurance*. It was indeed a colossal assurance of supe-
riority which Richelieu bestowed on France.

He built France at home: did he build well? Critics
point out that the French monarchy went down in such
blood and terror as has overwhelmed few monarchies.
Richelieu built for Louis XIV; did he also build for the
Revolution? The answer is not simple. The flaws in his

dictatorship—its deplorable finance, its truncation of the growth of all popular institutions—brought about the latter end of the French monarchy. But the inefficiency of later governments and their failure to remedy the natural decay which in time afflicts all political systems were more to blame than his errors, some of which might have been rectified. Yet Richelieu's creation was an artificial system, not a natural growth rooted in the past history of France. If he did not work out an exact and original plan, he deliberately rejected and selected always with the idea of government from above. This necessity, and not the nature of existing or healthy French institutions, governed his decisions. Such systems are, of their very nature, sterile. Could Richelieu have made a more vital, more natural unity for France had he considered more generously, and with a loftier end than mere efficiency, her institutions as he found them? The question seems unanswerable. All that we know is that he did not try.

He built France abroad: did he build well? Critics of his foreign policy have sometimes been unfair. By weakening the periphery of the Germanic Empire, they argue, he made way for the growth of Prussia. He strengthened France's eastern frontier but in such a way as to call into being the very power which afterwards destroyed her. The year 1648 found its retribution in 1870. The argument is too far-fetched. No one in Richelieu's time could reasonably have foreseen the rise of Prussia, then a remote and wretched state, wasted in wars, despised by all. There were many stopping places between 1648 and 1870 when statesmen in a better position than Richelieu to guess the future might have taken steps to prevent the growth of the menacing giant in the East. Foreign policy should be conducted with foresight, but it cannot be conducted in anticipation of events far beyond the human horizon.

The worst that can be said of his achievement was that he strangled the popular voice of France in order to strengthen the authority of the King at home and abroad. But was there in France in the seventeenth century any voice that would have spoken so clearly for France to the world as the royal voice was made to do by Richelieu? The answer is that there was not. He built for his own time, thinking, as he himself expressed it, that "the salvation of the state is now or never." In one sense he was not right, for the salvation of the state in one epoch may be its destruction in the next. Richelieu built for France the stable and powerful monarchy which gave her a long preeminence among nations, rich to herself and fruitful for the culture of Europe. But the stable and powerful monarchy failed in its office, had not the power of change and renewal, and became corrupt and irresponsible. And when it fell its fall embittered and contaminated French politics for many generations.

The arguments which have arisen and will yet arise over the character and work of Richelieu are endless. He himself foresaw the criticisms of future statesmen with as much indifference as he looked on those of his contemporaries. "Those who work for the State," he had written, "should imitate the stars. The dogs bark, but they shine none the less and revolve in their courses."

Notes on Books

The massive biography of Richelieu planned by Gabriel Hanotaux in the last years of the nineteenth century was carried on and completed after his death by the Duc de la Force; the sixth and last volume appeared in Paris in 1947. The almost equally massive *Richelieu et la monarchie absolue*, by Avenel, in four volumes (Paris, 1884-90), concerns the state and administration of France more than the biography of the Cardinal. Carl Burckhardt's *Richelieu*, of which a good English translation appeared in 1940, was also planned on the grand scale but only the first volume has appeared, covering the Cardinal's rise to power.

Those interested in the Richelieu family background and the Cardinal's cultural activities should consult the various short studies and monographs by Louis Battifol. The standard work on Father Joseph is that by G. Fagniez (Paris, 1894) but the study by Aldous Huxley, *Grey Eminence* (London, 1941), brings out some interesting aspects of Father Joseph's character and outlook. On the Cardinal's economic policy the important work of Henri Hauser, *La Pensée et l'action économique du Cardinal de Richelieu* (Paris, 1944) is indispensable, but Franklin C. Palm, *The Economic Policies of Richelieu* (University of Illinois, 1920), and J. U. Nef, *Industry and Government in France and England 1540-1640* (Philadelphia, 1940), are useful.

For administrative questions the detailed work of Mousnier, *La Venalité des Offices sous Henri IV et Louis XIII* (Rouen,

147

1947), is valuable. For the Navy there is René de la Bruyère, *La Marine de Richelieu* (Paris, 1958). For the diplomatic history of the period there are two studies by Auguste Leman, *Urbain VIII et la Rivalité de la France et de la Maison d'Autriche* (Lille, 1920) and *Richelieu et Olivares* (Lille, 1938).

General works on the period are, in French, Lavisse, *Histoire de France*, Volume VI, Part II, covering the reign of Louis XIII. It is by Mariéjol, and although it is now in some respects out of date it is still useful. Another old but useful book is Jacques Boulenger, *Le Grande Siècle* (Paris, 1911). It is available in English as *The Seventeenth Century* (London, 1920). The best recent work is V. L. Tapié, *La France de Louis XIII et de Richelieu* (Paris, 1952), a compact, scholarly and comprehensive volume, which includes a helpful bibliography.

For the European background there is Henri Hauser, *La Préponderance Espagnol 1559-1660* (Paris, 1933) and G. Pagés, *La Guerre de Trente Ans* (Paris, 1939). In English the best general works on the European seventeenth century are those by David Ogg, W. F. Reddaway and G. N. Clark. For French intervention in the Thirty Years War there is the second volume of Michael Roberts, *Gustavus Adolphus* (London, 1958), and my own book on the Thirty Years War (London, 1938). The relevant volume of the new *Cambridge Modern History* is, at the time of writing (1962), still in preparation.

Richelieu's letters and despatches can be studied in the handsome eight-volume edition by Avenel (Paris, 1853-77). The standard edition of his *Mémoires* is that begun under the auspices of the *Société de l'Histoire de France* in 1907. The best edition of the *Testament Politique* is that by Louis André (Paris, 1947).

Index